For the Children's Sake

For the Children's Sake

Foundations of Education for Home and School

Susan Schaeffer Macaulay

Foreword by Fiona Macaulay-Fletcher

:: CROSSWAY®

WHEATON, ILLINOIS

Published in association with the Child Light Limited. For more information concerning the educational resources of Child Light, see page 199.

The publisher wishes to thank the World Education Service (WES) for giving permission to quote from Charlotte Mason's books. WES continues the work Charlotte Mason founded in 1887. In fact, PNEU (Parents' National Education Union) remains the official title of the organization as an educational charity and as a company limited by guarantee. It provides a range of services which are largely used by English-speaking expatriates living outside the United Kingdom. Its long established and widely respected Home School Service (endorsed by the Department of Education and Science, London) enables parents to educate their own children. WES also helps to set up and run British-style schools overseas, as well as providing related services. Its address is: World Education Service, Waverley House, Penton, Carlisle, Cumbria, England, CA6 5QU.

Cover design: Josh Dennis
Cover image: Laughing Elephant, The Stapleton Collection/Bridgeman Images
Reprinted with new cover 2009
Second edition printed 2022
Printed in the United States of America

Trade paperback ISBN: 978-1-4335-8000-0
ePub ISBN: 978-1-4335-8003-1
PDF ISBN: 978-1-4335-8001-7
Mobipocket ISBN: 978-1-4335-8002-4

Library of Congress Catalog Card Number 83-72043

Crossway is a publishing ministry of Good News Publishers.

BP		31	30	29	28	27	26	25	24	23	22
15	14	13	12	11	10	9	8	7	6	5	4	3	2	1

This book is dedicated with love to
Ranald, Margaret, Kirsteen, Fiona, and Ranald John.
Each, a friend, a joy:
Together, one family.
With thanks to our Lord who makes abundant life possible.

Contents

Foreword

WHAT IS IT ABOUT *For the Children's Sake* that has continued to make it such a firm favorite? It was written by my mother in 1983, when I was thirteen, and it has remained in print ever since. First and foremost, it has inspired its readers and helped them discover the depth and richness of Charlotte Mason's philosophy of education. Many were disillusioned by utilitarian and reductionist approaches, and they were hungry for something more holistic. *For the Children's Sake* provided the inspiration and direction they needed. They began to appreciate Charlotte Mason's focus not so much on the acquisition of skills and facts but upon cultivating the "life of the mind." In turn, my mother's book prompted the republication of Charlotte Mason's six volumes (including *A Philosophy of Education*); many were inspired to start homeschooling their children; some founded new schools; a vast array of educational resources was spawned; and Charlotte Mason conferences were held. Unwittingly, my mother initiated a new educational movement—the last thing she expected.

Her first contact with Charlotte Mason's writings came when I was just a toddler. My two older sisters had started at the PNEU School in Compton, Sussex. For them and for her, it was like coming home: the threads of her own childhood, nurtured in a rich home environment, came together in this coherent and satisfying philosophy. It echoed all that had been modeled for her by her parents: a love of the arts, a love of music and nature, a love of books; all involving the sharing of ideas and held together within a Christian framework and enriched by lots of discussion. It simply made sense to her from what she knew was rich about life and true of children.

Charlotte Mason's first principle is that "the child is a person"—to which the response might be, "Well, of course: isn't that obvious?" Actually, this seems far from obvious, and many educational practices and children's toys and merchandise make this only too apparent. They speak down to the child. In the subject of history, for example, when five- or six-year-olds have the capacity and hunger for real history, they might be patronized in a typical school in the UK with topics such as "Toys Past and Present." In a similar way, gimmicky "kids" programs and toys so often fail to satisfy. They lack the ingredients that are necessary for a child's proper growth, that is, for the feeding of the mind and fostering of the imagination. Far from respecting children the gimmicks end up limiting them. As persons, they deserve more.

In practice though, does her methodology really work in the twenty-first century? Within a modern-day approach to teaching, do things like narration and living books, or her theory of education as the science of relations, still have relevance? Charlotte Mason saw that they worked. She saw, too, the central importance of cultivating intrinsic motivation: the joy of learning and doing one's best is itself the reward. As an educator I have seen these simple but hugely powerful methodologies, along with their undergirding philosophy, work over the last fourteen years in a school we founded on Charlotte Mason's principles. We have seen that pupils—whose foundations have been deeply laid on "books and things," using narration to lock their knowledge in place, and who learn not for marks and prizes but because learning is its own reward—are set up to flourish as lifelong learners. Our modern distracted, driven, and anxious children need this inheritance more than ever.

Why has *For the Children's Sake* resonated with so many people over so many years? To me the answer is straightforward: I can't count how many people I have met, both parents and educators, who say it simply "makes sense" of what they know to be true of the child and education. It goes with the grain of who we are. This is why we can be confident that Charlotte Mason's educational vision will stand the test of time.

Fiona Macaulay Fletcher

2021

Acknowledgments

THIS IS A BOOK that was lived first, however poorly, and then written. It's really Ranald's book; he often urged me to get on with the job of writing the ideas down. So thank you, Ranald; without you there *really* wouldn't have been a book to share! Thanks also to our children: Margaret, Kirsteen, Fiona, and Ranald John. You constantly teach me new lessons, open up new ideas. Thanks also to the other children who have inspired these pages, especially Jeremy, Stephen, and Peter Boddington; Christopher, Timmy, and Benjamin Keyes; Peter, Paul, and Philip Barrs; Johanna, Matthew, Rebecca, and Triana Winter; and Andrew, Joanne, and Fiona Seagren.

I also thank the many who discussed ideas about children, education, and life over the last years. Thanks to people who have already tried out aspects of this work in inner-city schools and camps. Thank you, Olive Norton, for introducing us to Charlotte Mason in the first place. Thank you, L'Abri workers, who allowed me time and gave support.

The advice, encouragement, and practical help of Jerry Nims, Franky Schaeffer, and Joan Molyneux are appreciated. Thank you.

Ideas aren't any use without the practical backup! Thank you, Christine Purvis and Pam Hendry, for typing; David Porter for editing; Ray Cioni for a delightful cover design; and Lane Dennis for publishing!

A very special thank you to my parents, Francis and Edith Schaeffer. You gave *me* much of this child-life, and this book grew from the life you nurtured. Your work forms the basis of these considerations. Your combined books are surely the base of this philosophy and practice of education. Your great love and concern for children and young people encouraged us to try to be of some practical help to others. Thank you for your interest, love, suggestions, and prayers that supported us throughout.

Introduction

I'D LIKE TO EXPLAIN a couple of things to you before you start this book.

When I began writing it, I used the phrase "he or she" when talking about people in general. I did so because I wanted to make it clear that boys and girls and men and women are included when we talk about persons.

Unfortunately, it became very awkward when spelled out each time, and it might well have become a real hindrance to readers. So in later drafts I reluctantly went back to the old-fashioned "he," intending it to mean "he or she" just as "man" conventionally means "man and woman."

I do hope that this compromise doesn't give offense to any reader. It's a question of simplifying language, not of devaluing my own sex. I'm not giving male children a higher status than female, nor male adults a higher status than females. I believe that all are of equal value, and I believe that this is the Bible's teaching.

Another point I would like to make is that this book takes the accuracy of the Christian worldview for granted, without first making out a case for it being true.

Now, my reason for believing that the Bible is true is not simply because I've been a Christian since childhood. Quite the contrary. It's very important to me that there are reasons why the Judeo-Christian faith can be seen to be actually true. It's just that this is not the book in which to explain those reasons.

I'm starting from the time when, as ordinary parents, my husband Ranald and I tried to find a practical educational philosophy. For us, this had to relate to the truth of Christianity. However, you'll find lots of ideas that are often put into practice by many thoughtful non-Christians! Of course, if we stumble upon things that are really right, we'll not be the only ones who will have noticed them. Good and true ideas keep cropping up in different contexts. If you aren't a Christian, you'll still be fascinated by this human, balanced, practical view of what education and life is all about.

One last consideration. This book devotes quite a lot of space to the work of Charlotte Mason, an educationalist who lived some time ago. Many of the books and materials she worked with will seem very old-fashioned today. It may be that, either from the extracts quoted herein or from an examination of the materials themselves in your local library or bookshop, you will decide that your twentieth-century children will never want to read them. That may be true (and it may be equally true that once they have been encouraged to *really* read, they will find many new friends on Charlotte Mason's bookshelf). But please, don't throw out the ideas along with the materials. This book can be applied to people's lives anywhere, at any time. It is not a specific guide to one particular plan. There are many books in print today which Charlotte Mason would certainly have enjoyed using. Education is an adventure that has to do with central themes, not the particular packages a given generation puts them into. It's about people, children, life, reality!

1

What Is Education?

OUR FIRST CHILD was growing up in London, and as school age approached we began the search for education. As young parents we wanted the best for our curly-headed toddler. But what *was* the best?

We visited schools and imagined our daughter living out her child life in them. We reacted instinctively. It couldn't be the school where the desks were so crowded that an adult couldn't walk through the room. And would we be satisfied with the school where a teacher had told a friend that it was so noisy she didn't try to teach reading? We were further discouraged when this same lady later said, "I can't remember the children's names. Who is Ruth?"

Could we imagine our creative, singing Margaret sitting in a desk memorizing facts from morn to night? Or would we be satisfied with the opposite, the noisy chaos of endless free play?

This is a problem many parents face. What should we aim for when thinking about education? We want the best, but when we look around at what's available, we often have to settle for situations that we would not have chosen in the first place.

When we tried to figure out guidelines in education, we couldn't find a practical overview of the subject. We invited experts to lecture to groups, but somehow it didn't help.

Well, Margaret had the best we could find, and all went well until we moved. The school near our new home turned out to be a blight on our youngster's life. Why? One reason was that the program of learning just didn't fit this particular child. Although we hadn't been able to organize an overall understanding of the subject, by now we were experienced enough parents to realize that something was badly wrong; drastic action had to be taken. We took Margaret out of school. Suddenly our child revived. She read books, played in the garden, worked alongside of us, enjoyed music. But an inspector didn't feel this education was satisfactory. Margaret should be in school. At that time, we didn't realize that he was wrong. The law in England allows for "education otherwise than at school." Eleven years later, Margaret's younger brother and sister were able to enjoy home-based education. But at that earlier time we sadly accepted that in the law's eyes "education" equals a schoolroom. In this case it meant two frustrating years, with forty children to one teacher. Was this what a child's life was meant to be? A drive to a closed-off cement area, a crowded room, a day so tiring that at the end Margaret and her younger sister came home taut with exhaustion?

We did the best we could in the hours spent away from school. But our prayers were becoming pretty desperate. And then, unexpectedly, the answer came.

The end of that story must wait to be told later in this book. Suffice it to say that the answers came when we found a little school run in a cottage. After our children went there, we realized that here was something really different. What was it? It seemed that the school still practiced the gentle art of an education based on a certain Charlotte Mason's ideas. We were, quite frankly, impressed. Could we find out more about these educational ideas? Was this what we were looking for?

We sent off for books (now out of print) by this lady who lived nearly a hundred years ago. I can remember how we sat in bed reading, often stopping to share some newly discovered concept. Our enthusiasm grew. The ideas made such good sense! We found that they are relevant to today's child and today's society. They are of such universal nature that one can apply them equally well at home, in different kinds of schools, in an orphanage in Africa, in an Indian village, in an inner-city school or day care center.

The ideas are so true that many of them are instinctively used by those with different educational or religious systems. They give us a satisfying view of education, or a child's life, from a Christian viewpoint. They provide a framework.

Before we continue with a consideration of these ideas I ought to introduce you to Charlotte Mason.

Charlotte Mason

Charlotte Mason (1842–1923) was no armchair philosopher. Her views were shaped by her teaching experiences, not the other way around. She first decided that teaching was to be her life's work when she was still a child and saw a young teacher with a class of poor children. Neither did she ever consider that she had arrived at a final, authoritative "last word" in the field of education. There is a striking lack of pride in the title of her final book: *An Essay Towards a Philosophy of Education.*

A modest view of her own achievements, however, was not accompanied by any timidity when it came to putting her ideas into practice. Charlotte Mason believed passionately that children are *persons* who should be treated as individuals as they are introduced to the variety and richness of the world in which they live. She believed that biblical Christianity is truth. She had a pivot, a foundation.

Her determination was tested to the full at the age of sixteen by the sudden death of her parents. In the face of personal grief, she persisted in her ambition and was successful in securing a place in the only teacher training college in England at that time. It was the beginning of an impressive, pioneering achievement which has a place in the history of women's contributions to society. But she was not able to remain a student for long. Probably because of the pressures of her financial situation, she obtained, after only a year at the college, a job as the teacher of a small school in Worthing. She managed to continue her studies in her spare time, as well as recording her experiences and thoughts. The year 1863 brought her the welcome award of a First Class certificate based on her work.

She really loved the children she taught. They were not just interesting specimens or an intriguing challenge. From the very start, they were valued friends, persons whom she respected. And this in a generation when children were normally meant to be "seen and not heard."

When the Bishop Otter College in Chichester appointed her as vice principal in 1874, Charlotte Mason had the chance to prepare lectures on the subject of education. Four years later ill health forced her to give up the post, and it seemed that her contribution to educational thought was destined to die an early death.

The enforced leisure was useful, however, as it gave time for further study and observation. Her thoughts crystallized into broad, helpful outlines. These she expressed in a series of lectures to parents. They found them so helpful that a National Society of Parents devoted to these ideas was started. Publications, journals, and finally specific curriculum guides gained wide and eager acceptance. Some parents were already teaching their children at home, but soon some families banded together to form schools. These were the famous Parents' National Education Union schools (after this referred to as PNEU schools). One thing led to another. Charlotte Mason opened a House of Education at Ambleside in the English Lake District. This was a college for young women training to be teachers. Many found their first taste of true education for themselves as they prepared to teach others.

To begin with, the children whose parents followed Charlotte Mason's teaching were those of the educated classes themselves. But Charlotte Mason never forgot her first vision. She asked all parents who had been helped to organize meetings and so pass on the ideas to the mothers who would never be reached through her books. Perhaps her greatest joy was when numbers of underprivileged children had the richness of her school curriculum and practices applied in their overcrowded and underfunded schools. She delighted in the awakening of these previously dimmed minds. Children became fluent speakers and lovers of literature and art. Her vision was that these good wholesome aspects of life would bring joy, stability, and richness to every child.

By the time of her death in 1923, she had written several excellent books. She was the founder of an important educational movement and of a family of schools that touched countless young lives. She had started and led a "house of education" that had trained many students, not only for teaching, but also for living an abundant life. Through her work, families had been strengthened and guided in their life and purpose.

What happened? Why have so few heard of her today? Why do so few remember that she was one of the great educationalists, one who changed the whole idea of what education is and how we can go about it? I believe one reason is that the strong Christian base upon which she built became unpopular. The view of what life is all about, changed. In fact, our generation cannot grasp the key that explains exactly what human life is. Children have often been the chattels of the adults. Their worth is constantly expressed in terms of dollars and cents, their education in terms of their being a cog in a machine, to be made fit for the highest paid job possible.

What a tragedy.

Christians can't develop a Christian view of education by accepting the usual aims and views of our society and then adding a "Christian message" or interpretation.

No, we start from a different *basis*. We have another worldview, another *people* view!

When a baby is picked up, spoken to, and loved, he is starting his education as God planned it. For all our lives we are human beings, in an active state of learning, responding, understanding. Education extends to all of life. In fact, an educational system that says, one bright summer's day in the dawn of my youth, "There. Now you are educated. This piece of paper says so," is doing me a gross disfavor. The truly educated person has only had many doors of interest opened. He knows that life will not be long enough to follow everything through fully.

This broad view of true education as the sum of all of life meant that Charlotte Mason first turned her attention to the parents. She believed that they had the most interesting and valuable vocation that exists amongst mankind. Into their love, care, and responsibility this person was placed. Charlotte Mason never spoke of education as merely taking place behind the walls of the schoolroom. She saw the home as the basic educational environment.

There will be different applications of these ideas for different families. Families have to consider the educational system they are actually up against. More than that, different children within one family may need different decisions as to what educational system is best for them. And it is important to apply Jesus's teaching that we must not judge other peoples' choices. Just because I decide to send my little Tom to the local public school or a private Christian school, or because I decide to give him a home education, does not mean that everyone else has to do the same. It is a complicated situation. Consider this: the average American child (and the British child doesn't lag too far behind) spends more time in front of the TV than he ever spends at school. Many teenagers cull most cultural norms from their peers and all forms of media. I am not saying that school is not tremendously important. However, school is only *one* of the influences in children's lives. It can often be that a strong, rich home life with Christian teaching and understanding more than offsets the "center of gravity" at a secular school.

Involvement by parents and teachers working in the secular institutions, private and public, is right. Voice and action are often the needed salt a situation requires to make it better rather than worse. Some schools are like cesspools spiritually, mentally, and/or physically. Jesus said we were not to place a stumbling block in front of the child. Some schools are nothing but stumbling blocks. The end product is neither an educated person, nor one who has had a chance as a moral and free human being.

This is why many feel that something urgent has to be done. It may be simple: a family with their own children delighting in learning and living right at home without "going to school." It may be a group of families who get together to share a very simple structure of community school living. It may be known as a Christian school. It may be someone who has a vocation to help the abandoned children of our urban ghettos, or those emotionally disturbed due to unsettled backgrounds. Surely caring for such children should be seen as a moral issue of the utmost urgency by the Christian citizens of our countries.

Any choice and/or arrangement should be done for the children's sake. We are told in Galatians 6:9–10, "Let us not become weary in doing good, for at the proper time we will reap a harvest if we do not give up. Therefore, as we have opportunity, *let us do good to all people* [children are people], *especially to those who belong to the family of believers.*"

Also, consider the Gospel of Matthew. First of all we must humbly ask for answers, we must seek, and then, "Knock and the door will be opened to you. For everyone who asks receives; he who seeks finds; and to him who knocks, the door will be opened" (Matt. 7:7–8).

Surely this basic principle includes that broad lifelong seeking in all areas. Thank God that there is a definite answer! We are not only seekers but finders.

The passage continues, "Which of you, if his son asks for bread, will give him a stone? Or if he asks for a fish, will give him a snake? If you, then, though you are evil, know how to give *good gifts* to your children, how much more will your Father . . ." (Matt. 7:9–11).

Children ask for bread. Do we give them white gummy glue covered with saturated fat? Do we feed their bodies on any careless prepacked junk that comes into view? Or do we provide them with honest good food?

And what about their minds, their spirits? Do we make those bright eager eyes focus on any old, canned, mental junk food? Do we brush off the eager questions, and then expect the children to listen to some "spiritual lecture" another time?

Where to start? How? Parents need to evaluate their priorities. They need to consider *why* they respond, "We wouldn't have time to read a book together every day. We don't have time to hike/camp/paint/talk with our children." What is really important? The sacred career? Educational institutions make poor substitute mothers, fathers, and homes. There has never been a generation when children have so desperately needed their parents' time, thoughtful creativity, and friendship. The surrounding culture is deeply out of step with the word of God. Other pressures threaten to take away sanity, stability, and simple humanity.

One of the greatest powers for good is a family whose members respect each other and who have learned to function, however poorly, with the rich concepts the word of God gives us as human beings. It is almost incredible to think of the stabilizing effect ordinary families can have: not only for themselves, but as a light in a troubled generation.

Another application of Charlotte Mason's ideas would be for the person who is working with children in any setup at all. Children can come to their public school teachers as to a stable adult friend in a personally insecure world. You need never speak a specific Christian word to them (although this is a sad limitation), and yet can help them *as persons*. Even a glimmer of light can transform a dark world. The ideas will be applicable in a church or Christian community where the basic principles may play their part. How about a babysitter using them? I know of someone who did, with quite astonishing results. Then there is day care and after-school care. Or how about being a friendly neighbor who gives the gift of helping that child who has nobody with time for *him*? How about your nieces, nephews, grandchildren?

I would appeal also to the single person. Please don't walk by on the other side. Christian single persons are in the position of having extra flexibility. Children in need are in every church, school, and community. They are often emotionally adrift, without that sweet and natural security of their parents' marriage to give a base to their family life. Parents become tense and stressed, trying to fit fast-moving careers into ordinary human life. Schools become mechanical, where the child all too often doesn't really count. TV becomes a sedative, stilling active play, reading, talking, sharing. Planned activities crowd out personal growth and creativity. And the god of money, status, and personal ease and pleasure seeps in everywhere, like a noxious gas.

If Christianity is indeed true, then every last little child matters. Bright to dull, privileged or from any variety of troubled background, each is valuable. *Persons matter*.

Let us really and truly be courageous. Much of what follows goes against the daily pattern of most lives. It's interesting to read about, but it will remain as so many words on a page if we cannot do what we know is right. One day we will stand before the Creator. Were we willing to give, serve, and sacrifice *"for the children's sake"*?[1]

2

"Children Are Born Persons"

THIS FIRST PROPOSITION of Charlotte Mason's educational phi-losophy may seem merely a statement of the obvious. But I want to emphasize that it is not some minor element of a greater truth. It is a central truth in its own right, and if we ignore it, great sorrow and malpractice can result.

Try a simple experiment. Take a small child on your knee. Respect him. Do not see him as something to prune, form, or mold. This is an individual who thinks, acts, and feels. He is a separate human being whose strength lies in who he is, not in who he will become. If his choices made now and in the future are to be good ones, this person must understand reality and see the framework of truth. In the shorthand of language we call this "knowing." The child is a person who needs to grow in knowledge.

You have some of that knowledge. Not because you are an adult and adults are supposed to be wonderfully clever; the Bible is very clear in its teaching that there is a sense in which we must ourselves become like this little child on our knee if we are to inherit the kingdom of God. But we have knowledge because we have lived in God's world as persons, and that knowledge can be shared. Christians have the added perspective of God's word from which to explain their experience and understanding of life.

We are told by many in our generation that this small child is a cog in a machine, or even that he is a possession, like a pet animal. Many adults now "have" a child, in the same way that they "have" a washing machine or a collie dog.

We must answer: No. You are holding a *person* on your knee. And that is wonderful.

What sort of person is it whom we are holding? To know him we must consider the various aspects integrated into the unity which we call "this person" (Johnny, Sally).

Physically, his little body may be vigorous and healthy or malnourished and dejected. His mind may be alert and responsive, or it may be dulled and neglected. His emotions may be warm, trusting, affectionate or fearful, wary and suspicious because of past hurt. His spirit may be awake to that great Lover of children, or it may be ignorant and withdrawn. Worse, he may already be bored by sawdust-like religious slogans. Has he been warmed at the flame of the Shepherd who has cared for *him*?

Look well at the child on your knee. In whatever condition you find him, look with reverence. We can only love and serve him and be his friend. We cannot own him. He is not ours.

Neither would it be right to use the fact that he is dependent on us to brainwash him into thinking any arbitrary thought or perform any arbitrary act that we may deem useful. We should not plan his life for him, so that he is being prepared for some great purpose—even if the purpose we intend is a worthy one in our eyes (such as becoming an ever-loyal and patriotic supporter of our own denomination or brand of politics, or acting out our own ego, pride, or ambition). This was an important issue for Charlotte Mason.

> We must know something about the material we are to work upon if the education we offer is not to be scrappy and superficial. We must have some measure of a child's requirements, not based on his uses to society, nor upon the standard of the world he lives in, but upon his own capacity and needs.[1]

Charlotte Mason rejects the utilitarian view of education and the conventional educational standards of her day. She challenges us instead to identify the child's *actual* needs and capacities, to serve him as he *is*, on the basis of what is right and good for him as a person.

Will this perspective not produce a selfish, nonuseful member of society? No indeed. Not if we serve this person with true education.

> Our journals ask with scorn, "Is there no education but what is got out of books at school? Is not the lad who works in the fields getting an education?" and the public lacks the courage to say definitely, "No, he is not," because there is no clear notion current as to what education means, and how it is to be distinguished from vocational training. But the people begin to understand and to clamor for an education which shall qualify their children for life rather than for earning a living. As a matter of fact, it is the person who has read and thought on many subjects who is, with the necessary training, the most capable whether in handling tools, drawing plans, or keeping books. *The*

more of a person we succeed in making a child, the better will he
both fulfil his own life and serve society.[2]

And so Charlotte Mason rejected the idea that what this young
person needed was *molding*. "Their notion is that by means of a
pull here, a push there, a compression elsewhere a person is at last
turned out according to the pattern the educator has in his mind."[3]

Charlotte Mason was, however, a realist. She accepted the little
child exactly as he was. She did not romanticize him, but she appreciated him and looked with wonder at what she found.

The most prosaic of us comes across evidence of mind in children, and of mind astonishingly alert. Let us consider, in the first
two years of life they manage to get through more intellectual
effort than any following two years can show. [She proceeds to
catalog the marvelous accomplishments that occur in the self-
education of these young persons under two.] . . . If we have not
proved that a child is born a person with a mind as complete and
beautiful as his little body, we can at least show that he always
has all the mind he requires for these occasions; that is, that his
mind is the instrument of his education and that his *education
does not produce his mind.*[4]

Can you sense the atmosphere in which this educator approached
children? *She respected their minds,* even as equally capable as her
own exceedingly capable mind. She used the term "twaddle" for the
mentally inferior and useless stuff produced or written for children
by adults. She saw that it devalued their minds.

I like both the word and the concept it communicates. I can
readily imagine the scene Charlotte Mason describes in her book

Home Education, a book written to help parents and teachers educate children under nine years of age.

> Indeed, I am inclined to question whether, in the interest of carrying out a system, the charming [kindergarten] teacher is not in danger sometimes of greatly undervaluing the intelligence of her children. I know a person of three who happened to be found by a caller alone in the drawing-room. It was spring, and the caller thought to make himself entertaining with talk about the pretty "baa-lambs." But a pair of big blue eyes were fixed upon him and a solemn person made this solemn remark, "Isn't it a dwefful howid thing to see a pig killed!" We hope that she had never even heard of the killing of a pig, but she made as effective a protest against twaddle as would any woman of Society. . . . Treasure Island, Robinson Crusoe and his man Friday, the fight of Thermopylae, Ulysses and the suitors—these are the sorts of things that children play at by the month together; even the toddlers of three or four will hold their own manfully with their brothers and sisters. And, if the little people were in the habit of telling how they feel, we should learn perhaps that they are a good deal bored by the nice little games in which they frisk like lambs, flap their fins, and twiddle their fingers like butterflies.[5]

This is one of the fundamental principles which made Charlotte Mason into a great educator. She not only *said* that she treasured a child's mind, but she acted upon that belief. It had many practical ramifications, as we shall see later on. Charlotte Mason enjoyed sharing the good things of life with the eager minds of children (this is an important concept which we will explore in more detail later in the book). She dealt with them on an eye-to-eye level. She never felt that they weren't old enough to appreciate and think about things which she knew were good. She delighted in introducing them to all aspects of reality, with a positive joy. She delighted in their separate individuality.

Twaddle. If I were to have to label much educational material today, I'm afraid a large percentage would definitely be twaddle. How colorfully and scientifically our generation talks down to the little child! What insipid, stupid, dull stories are trotted out! And we don't stop there. We don't respect the children's thinking or let them come to any conclusions themselves! We ply them with endless questions, the ones *we've* thought up, instead of being silent and letting the child's questions bubble up with interest. We tire them with workbooks that would squeeze out the last drop of anybody's patience. We remove interesting books and squander time on a clinical procedure called "reading skill testing," using idiotic isolated paragraphs which nobody would dream of choosing to take home to read. The recording of testable features of a child's taught tricks ("skills") is held to be more important than the mysterious, exciting growth of a *person.*

I feel profoundly sad that such things should be happening. It need not be so. As I write, I remember the bright brown eyes of another interesting person, at present aged four. A few weeks ago she was in a small group of children listening to a straightforward biblical narration of creation, of the first persons, and of their deliberate choice to disobey God's command. The children had been deeply attentive and interested. Suddenly the brown eyes flashed. "But, Susan, it isn't *true*, is it?"

How amazed and interested she was when I said that it was indeed true! People five times her age have asked the same question. I cannot see any essential difference. In both cases, it is an intelligent, basic question. Children's minds work as ours do.

When the story was over, the children left, unselfconscious and relaxed. Two weeks later, they retold me the entire story without one word of prompting.

They had been presented with straightforward history. It interested them, just as history interests adults. They had no need for a little twaddle talk at the end, to tell them how or what to think about what they had heard.

Suppose I had been ill-advised enough to say, "Sit still, Jenny, and don't bring up your ideas about truth right now. Today we are supposed to think about families. So we will think about mommies and daddies and that God made them so they would have a family right at the very beginning."

What would I have been doing?

After narrating one of the great history stories of all time, I would have been reducing its breadth and interest by telling the children what I thought they should think and feel about it.

There would have been several distinct consequences.

1. They would have been deprived of the chance to wonder at the story and to make their own personal response; they would have been deprived of the right to think.
2. The closing sermonette would most probably have degenerated into twaddle, thereby boring them. (And if they weren't bored then, I can assure you that they would be the third time it happened.)
3. I might have been tempted to capture their interest by other means than the deep fascination of the story. I might have tried to catch their eye with a set of puppets, perhaps.

4. Jenny would not have asked herself, "Is it true?" Her brown eyes wouldn't have sparkled with the answer—*truth*!

5. All the fancy additions to the story would have kept her mind from working by itself. It would also have taken a lot longer. Therefore the lesson would have kept her from a lovely twenty-minute scamper on the lawn with her friends.

We devalue the personhood of our wonderful children. We rob their minds of proper, interesting, strong meat to nourish their growing needs. We belittle their interests. We compete with the entertainment of TV. We flick images, flash colors, use tricks. And yet many small children are at the same time being robbed of free and happy childhood play. Endless "play-approach" lessons bore them and leave no time for imaginative *real* play in or out-of-doors.

"Johnny is hyper. Let's sedate him."

"Why are Jenny's eyes dulled? She doesn't seem to take any interest in our carefully thought-out talk, even though it is severely within the 'guidelines-of-the-vocabulary-and-concepts-understood-by-the-four-year-old.'"

"The idea of 'truth' will be talked about in junior high Sunday school, year 8, day 21."

Why do I feel so profoundly sad? Dear Lord, the little children are being smothered! They are often pinched, pushed, managed, and neglected into the bargain. The experience of beauty in God's great outdoors is often exchanged for seeing flickering images on a screen. Adults have so often stopped giving children time priority; they are relegated to the category of "menial jobs." Many regard them as positively horrible; they resent their intrusion into their time and pocketbooks. Dear God, where are the friends and lovers of children? Who will open up the wonderful windows onto the whole of reality and let their capable minds be stimulated? Who will accept them as they really are—as persons?

This is why I feel that this whole question is one of utmost urgency.

We have to be willing to start again.

Before we go any further, here is a challenge.

Get to know a child. It may be your own or somebody else's. Don't think of it as either a menial or a professional task. Do it for its *own* sake. I can assure you, the child will bring more to you than you can bring to him or to her. A child can be the very best friend in all the world. They are so responsive. Their minds are challenging and wonderfully surprising.

Get a few really good books, and read them together aloud. Set aside a good regular chunk of time. This will be one of the most rewarding and stimulating relationships in your life. Guess what? If you have the courage to be honest, that youngster's comments and questions are really going to make you think, think *hard*. You can throw away all the manuals. That child has an awful lot to teach you. Your mind is probably in a worse state than his. After reading together, go to a really nice place outside for a couple of hours at least. Don't rush. Turn a rock over and watch the beetles run away. Throw rocks in the stream and slide down a hill.

Talk together. You'll find yourself enjoying it! Relax.

It isn't all as hard as the experts make out. We are human beings, persons, created to *live*. To have life *more* abundantly. Wonder together; grow together. Together share the struggles of knowing that we cannot perfectly follow God's law. We are fellow-pilgrims. We walk side by side as human beings under the love and authority of Him who made us.

Applying Some Aspects of the Fact That Children Are Persons

If we have any insight at all, we will quickly identify the fact that Christians begin from a very different starting point when thinking about education. It is not merely a question of what we want to teach, who teaches it, or what exactly is right or wrong. It is deeper. We speak of who the human being is. We do not have to achieve anything to earn self-worth; we know that the person is a creature of this planet, into whom God breathed the spirit of personality. Yes, we are created having that within ourselves which is so unique that God could say, "'Let us make man in our own image' . . . Male and female created He them" (Gen. 1:26–27 KJV).

We know that the first persons made a wrong choice, that we live in an abnormal world. Yet the message of Christianity is about God's provision for me which, when followed, can give me a relationship with a God who is there, a measure of peace within myself, and meaningful relationships with other human beings around me. Last but not least, I am responsible for the planet on which I live and of which I am a part.

One aspect of life is not more Christian than another. So it's Christian to enjoy a juicy melon. That is because I am eating, it is a real event, and I'm made so that I enjoy cool melon on a hot day. It is Christian to put my arm around someone to love or comfort them. That is because this is a way human beings relate, show they care, enjoy each other. More than this: it must be said that certain Christian books are in fact not so. For instance, some go beyond biblical teaching and, like the Pharisees, burden the people with weighty rules and regulations. This is why we have to be very, very careful when we consider "Christian education." To be that, it has to serve the *person*, the way he really is. And it must, of course, be based on the sureness of the biblical truths. So it has to be appropriate for the *needs* and *minds* of that same person.

Play

I would think that as good a place as any to start is the concept of play. After the child's needs of love and nourishment are provided for, the child plays.

> There is a little danger in these days of much educational effort that children's play should be crowded out, or, what is from our present point of view the same thing, should be prescribed for and arranged until there is no more freedom of choice about play than about work. We do not say a word against the educational value of games (such as football, basketball, etc.) . . . But organised games are not *play* in the sense we have in view. Boys and girls must have time to invent episodes, carry on adventures, live heroic lives, lay sieges and carry forts, even if the fortress be an old armchair; and in these affairs the elders must neither meddle nor make.

She goes on to say that if we do organize their play there is a

> . . . serious danger. In this matter the child who goes too much on crutches never learns to walk.[6]

This is a point which needs to be considered further. Play seems so natural (just like anything which is attuned to reality). The phrase *child's play* is part of our language. It ought to mean that quality of spontaneity, imagination, wholehearted concentration, and joy which should mark all children at play.

But one of the saddest things I know is to watch students at L'Abri look at a group of children, involved for hours in satisfying play, and comment, "I've never seen children playing like that."

No? Then weep. Even childhood is robbed of the riches of humanness. It is appropriate to pause and think about that.

Helping a Child to Play

There are many reasons why children have been reduced to a point where they don't play with joy, initiative, and creativity. Often so far as their personality is concerned they are wheelchair cripples, too disabled even for crutches.

Restorative action means scheduling time, time which is not obviously "improving." Believe me, I'm not talking theoretically, but as a mother of four children whose ages cover various stages. School hours are like a monster (however excellent that school may be), gobbling up the child's treasure of time. Careful now! We only get to be a child once! For some children, there are more calls on time: gymnastics, music, swimming, extra spelling, French tutoring. And what about the church? However worthwhile each separate activity is, it is important to keep a check on how much of the child's time is being "organized," and make a wise and *balanced* choice of priorities. Children's *overall* needs should be thoughtfully considered.

Then there is another time-consuming monster: homework. Ya-ha! Thought all those hours at school were *over*?

And here comes the last straw. Most children spend more time parked in front of TVs than they spend doing anything else. Their minds are unfed, their imaginations unused, their bodies unexercised, their thoughts unexpressed and unheard.

Six-year-old children are as pressurized as executives. Children are being "fitted into" a streamlined schedule designed for the parents so *they* can cope with *their* pressures. Institutions herd children; out of necessity, they need to consider group control more than the child's needs.

And so, overentertained, pushed, pulled, and tidied up, often the child of today has the rich creative play-response crushed out. Sometimes the only thing his dulled eyes focus on is a premature adolescence which will release him from childhood.

I grew up, until the age of six and a half, in an old-fashioned American neighborhood. We had space to play—a vacant lot, dozens of yards, an alley, and shaded sidewalks. Grown-ups left us to ourselves to play for hours on end, whole days strung together. We didn't have to rush off all the time to do things that were "good" for us. The adults left the children free to play and to organize their own time. Mind you, they didn't disappear either. They were there, living and working in that neighborhood. There was always someone to go to when you needed help and to notice when we were bad. But they didn't meddle with our time.

Also, TV hadn't arrived to mesmerize people. Everybody had more freedom after their hours of work.

Cops and robbers. Mud pies. Scratches from climbing trees. Adventures on tricycles. One child stares at an ant carrying a crumb, and a few others start a club in a garage.

Certain factors encourage play. It is often easier homebased than institution-based. There should be space and lots of free time. Children need to be outdoors (for hours). They need to make noise, mess, and to have access to raw materials (old clothes for costumes, hats, tables to turn into camps, etc., etc.). They need privacy from intruding adults, but they need interested support in quarrels, thinking of another way around a problem, providing food, and, at the end, bringing the children tactfully back into the world where supper *is* ready, the camp has to be packed up, children are tired and ready for the soothing routine of evening stories.

Grown-ups need time if *their* life is to support this kind of play. The children have to matter more than the furniture (but children don't mind at all sticking to the boundaries). This means saying no to too many time-consuming activities both for adults and children. It means welcoming their friends, and sympathetically diverting others who will "spoil our game. We've just got to the *good* part" (said with feeling as a destructive two-year-old blundered into the "camp").

If children are already passive, and stare with glazed eyes at a TV screen, or wander about bored when not organized, try going somewhere else. Water is always stimulating for children; playing by a stream or beach is usually satisfying. Don't be afraid to say, "No TV until Friday when we'll all watch that show together and then turn the set off." Or how about enjoying a few years without the materialistic and secular influence of TV at all?

What about people in apartments? Raw material for play is also to be found here. Spread out an inviting array of dress-up clothes, LEGOs, play-dough, or a pile of old cardboard boxes.

What about schools? Charlotte Mason so believed in this principle of giving children time to play that she organized the lessons so that the child could finish them about halfway through the day. As we will go on to see, this was not because she devalued the time of learning. Quite otherwise: because she respected the children's minds so highly, she provided a truly liberal education for them at a very young age. She arranged for a broad curriculum. However, she knew that if attention was to be given fully, the child should have it contained in a length of time appropriate for them. Then they could turn their attention from mind-work to enjoying nature, art, play, handcrafts, and physical activity. She believed firmly that they should have free time at home, in ordinary surroundings; so her schools never gave homework.

She was very human. If I had a second childhood, I should like to be educated her way in school. To be respected as a person, to be provided for richly with ideas from outside, and yet to be left to develop myself, according to my own inner resources. All of this within the firm framework of reality. Skills mastered, and yet a feast of interesting ideas to which one could react in one's own way.

I know this deeply, as in fact my childhood did provide me with so many of these joys at home. I know it was very special to be able to enjoy the Swiss Alps just the way my own imagination prompted me. However, there is no such thing as the perfect environment in which a child can play. If we try to organize perfection, we fail the child. Part of life is to learn to accept the limitations of any given situation. We do our children a lifelong service if we help them to make the best of where they live and who they are. Children are great adaptors. They will often make the best of the less-than-perfect situation.

This consideration of their need to play, if applied, will mean different things to different families and schools. There is no one way. For one parent, it may mean giving up a career for some time to become a full-time parent. The child who goes from school to aftercare centers may never have the privacy and freedom he needs. It may mean someone else moves to the country or gets a house near a field. Another family may start to cut back on organized activities, so as to leave the children more free time. Others may have to allow for more mess and confusion, such as allowing a game in the clean house on a rainy day (a fort, perhaps, made out of all the chairs pushed together with blankets and food supplies at hand).

Schools may send children home earlier, if they and the families are united in purpose. If they are serving children whose homes cannot or will not provide it, they may design both time and space so as to provide for this basic need at school. Day-care centers, inner-city programs, camps, residential homes—all should try to serve the child's needs. Can we use our creativity to think of ways in which children can be given a good place to play, using their own ideas? Adults will also need imagination and effort. They need to consider the priority that free play has in a child's life. Do we want a generation of stunted children?

When we begin studying the *person*, the real child, we must serve who he *is*, not fit him into *our* schedules or plans. Part of this is allowing him play.

Living Ideas from Outside of the Child

Boredom has a stranglehold on many children's lives today. How can they be helped to escape from it? What steps can we take to ensure that the plaintive words "I'm *bored!*" are rarely heard?

For the truth of the matter is that babies and young children explore new experiences with tireless enthusiasm. A girl or boy has a mind which is hungry for ideas. The four-year-old is often full of eager questions. Any parent of a preschooler knows how frustrating it can be taking young children out for a walk through the park if you want to get anywhere fast. Their curiosity keeps stopping them. They kick stones, jump off logs, lie down flat to watch a beetle. In the same way, it is easy to be drawn into reading, "One more story. Please. Just *one* more," while bedtime recedes further and further away.

The children are hungry! They have an appetite for knowing and experiencing.

It is the strong, real world that interests them so much, where the unexpected can happen, and there is wonderful mystery.

Children have a voracious appetite and ability to learn in their first five years. Parents who provide for their growth will have enthusiastic, outgoing, and creative children. If their children are the reflective type, this will provide a depth which builds quiet confidence. Having been treated as persons, they are secure. This means they've been loved, respected, talked with, listened to, read to. They have shared experiences with the family and have had freedom to play alone and with friends. Such children will be eager to exploit life without a sense of boredom. They will think and express their thoughts. They are eagerly trying to master new skills.

Why does the school institution often blunt this interest?

The child at school, sooner or later, has "doing" changed to "mastering skills." Often he has his initiative subordinated to a schedule which has been worked out according to pragmatic factors other than his creativity and needs. He has to try to become interested in hours of listening to talking. There may be no time for *him* to talk or to express himself. Worse, the books provided are often weak, watery, and insipid. Charlotte Mason's comments in *Home Education* all too often still apply:

We . . . put into the children's hand lesson books with pretty pictures and easy talk, almost as good as storybooks; but we do not see that, after all, we are giving them . . . little pills of knowledge in the form of a weak and copious diluent. Teachers, and even parents, who are careful enough about their children's diet, are so reckless as to the sort of mental aliment offered to them, that I am exceedingly anxious to secure consideration for this question, of the lessons and literature for little people. [She is writing here about children under nine, but the principles are the same at any age.] . . . We see, then, that the children's lessons should provide material for their mental growth, should exercise the several powers of their minds, should furnish them with fruitful ideas, and should afford them with knowledge, really valuable for its own sake, accurate, and interesting, of the kind that the child may recall as a man with profit and pleasure.[7]

Later on in the same book, we see that she was indeed hitting the nail on the head. Have you ever met college professors who bewailed the standard of the incoming students' past education? How well are children from "uneducated homes" helped at school? Is a new world of literacy and understanding opened to them? Are they given new opportunities?

Children who are the products of the scheme which is described below do have a chance to achieve their potential. It is a plan based on the assumption that all children are persons and are waiting to have doors opened for them.

First, Charlotte Mason devoted many pages to outlining a most sensible plan for teaching reading, writing, and number work itself. The lessons are structured and fitted to the child's need. These are mechanical skills, and each step is mastered before the next is taken. Many learning difficulties would not arise if this sort of basic thought-out teaching service was provided to children when *they* were ready and at *their* level and speed.

Meanwhile, as we shall see later on, Charlotte Mason ensured that the child was read to. Not isolated little stories but really good books, chapter by chapter. Those fortunate pupils had stories about all sorts of things. Biographies of historical figures, works of literature, stories about faraway places, fables, stories about animals and birds. Always really good books, chosen carefully by the criterion that a book should be "really valuable for its own sake, accurate, and interesting, of a kind that the child may recall . . . with pleasure."

All this reading isn't crammed in. After just one story, the little child tells back what he has heard, in his own words. Charlotte Mason called this "narration." It is wonderful that the mind that has heard can now express the interest and knowledge in the child's own words. No prompting or questioning. No moralizing or sermons.

> The most common and the monstrous defect in the education of the day is that children fail to acquire the habit of reading. Knowledge is conveyed to them by lessons and talk, but the studious habit of using books as a means of interest and delight is not acquired. This habit should begin early; so soon as the child can read at all, he should read for himself, and to himself, history, legends, fairy tales, and other suitable matter. He should be trained from the first to think that one reading of any lesson is enough to enable him to narrate what he has read, and will thus get the habit of slow, careful reading, intelligent even when it is silent, because he reads with an eye to the full meaning of every clause.[8]

Narration is such an obvious, natural response to the enjoyable experience of reading. I believe that that is why it works like magic.

Try it for yourself. Read the child a good tale, full of interest. Then say to him, "Can you tell me the story?" As he puts it into words, he has to think for himself. He uses his memory, and he is attending deeply. But his own reactions and expressions are involved. It is a total human activity. You don't need to reduce the child's appreciation to elementary "true/false" tests. The child has acquired knowledge, and having expressed it creatively in his own words, he will be able to remember what he has learned.

Educationalists replying to such arguments today will often agree that there is great value in reading but will point to the large numbers of books used in education as resource material; children have perfectly adequate access to books, it is often maintained. But that is not the same thing. It was Charlotte Mason's conviction that the child should work steadily through a complete book. Little snippets of information here and there just don't hang together. Our generation is prone to amuse itself with fragmentary information and resources. We flip on the TV for brief programs, and then we think we *know* about the subjects they dealt with. A few paragraphs in a magazine, and we think we've formed an opinion. What is happening so often is that we are merely forming a habit of amusing our interest and then forgetting the fragments. This is not education.

Children benefit from working steadily through a well-chosen book. And if they narrate it to you, it will become theirs. But more happens. Because they've tackled a complete book, they become acquainted with its flow and its use of language. They are students of another person—the author. Further, they are allowed to notice the content themselves. As they aren't forced to memorize facts, they are free to react to the writing themselves. They are the ones who decide what parts they consider important. It becomes an active experience of the mind, personality, and language.

The tiny child loves to be read to. Later on, he'll master the art of reading on his own. Then he'll be ready to read some of the "real" books for himself. The age that this happens can vary between four and nine or ten years.

He should have practice, too, in reading aloud, for the most part, in the books he is using for his term's work. These should include a good deal of poetry, to accustom him to the delicate shades of meaning, and especially to make him aware that words are beautiful in themselves, that they are a source of pleasure, and are worthy of our honour: and that a beautiful word deserves to be beautifully said, with a certain roundness of tone and precision of utterance. . . . In this connection the teacher should not trust to setting, as it were, a copy in reading for the children's imitation. They do imitate readily enough, catching tricks of emphasis and action in an amusing way; but these are mere tricks, an aping of intelligence. The child must express what *he* feels to be the author's meaning; and this sort of intelligent reading comes only from the habit of reading with understanding.[9]

Observe that Charlotte Mason has respected the child's ability to find the meaning and express himself, without a middleman.

"Literary Power"

The next point is so important that we shall consider it in several ways.

The child needs books with "literary power." We do not live in a generation which in practice sets much value on the enjoyment or expression of literary power. If C. S. Lewis, J. R. R. Tolkien, the apostle Paul, Shakespeare, Wordsworth, and Carl Sandburg, for instance, should have the unlikely experience of being in a typical school for several days, would they find any enjoyment in the material read by and to the third grade? The sixth, eighth, eleventh grades? Would they be able to enjoy a relationship with fascinating growing persons? Would they enjoy the family's reading before bed every evening? Or the conversation around the supper table? Would they perhaps be fascinated and stimulated by spending a month of Sundays in each Sunday school class, at each level?

If not, *why not?*

In all probability our distinguished visitors would hate the entire experience. Their minds would wander to the clouds floating outside the window. They would play truant mentally and/or physically.

There are two reasons why.

1. They would hate the endless restrictions and meaningless, time-consuming rituals, the lack of time to do things *they* want. They would hate being shut away from the outdoors and the cheerful give-and-take of people at ease with each other.

2. They would be depressed by twaddle. We have never been so rich in books. But there has never been a generation when there is so much twaddle in print for children, much of it in schools. Many school "readers," textbooks, colorful picturebooks, and Sunday school papers make a poor contrast to the magnificence of words such as "In the beginning God created the heavens and the earth." Why not keep our imaginary visitors' works as a standard? Consider Lewis, Tolkien, Paul, Shakespeare, Wordsworth, and Sandburg.

A child has not begun his education until he has acquired the habit of reading to himself, with interest and pleasure, books fully on a level with his intelligence. I am speaking now of his lessonbooks, which are all too apt to be written in a style of insufferable twaddle, probably because they are written by persons who have never chanced to meet a child.[10] All who know children know that they do not talk twaddle and do not like it, and prefer that which appeals to their understanding. Their lesson-books should offer matter for their reading, whether aloud or to themselves; therefore they should be written with literary power. As for the matter of these books, let us remember that children can take in ideas and principles, whether the latter be moral or mechanical, as quickly and clearly as we do ourselves (perhaps more so); but detailed processes, lists and summaries, blunt the edge of a child's delicate mind. Therefore, the selection of their first lesson-books is a matter of grave importance, because it rests with these to give children the idea that knowledge is supremely attractive and that reading is delightful. Once the habit of reading his lesson-books with delight is set up in a child, his education is not completed, but ensured; *he will go on for himself in spite of the obstructions which school too commonly throws in his way.*[11]

Charlotte Mason understood that knowing given lists of facts parrot-wise is not even the beginning of education. She satisfied the *minds* of young persons with substantial, interesting, well-written material that they could think about. She let them enjoy beauty in nature, writing, art, music, and the Bible as God's word to them. She left them precious childhood hours free to climb trees, explore woods, walk, ride, what have you.

In education, fashions come and go. What is beautiful about Charlotte Mason's view is that it corresponds to the way things really are. It aims to provide the child with a balanced approach in which his various needs will be met; he will be able to know objective truths and form relationships within life. Charlotte Mason respected the unity of the person: mind, soul (or spirit), and his physical self. Everything comes under the direction of the Great Giver of all wisdom and life, the Holy Spirit.

As we will see, she believed that education *had* to include the proper use of books. She said that reading the Bible directly and systematically would in itself educate the mind. But she made wide and varied use of literary books covering every field. That is what she meant by a liberal education.

She expected a lot from quite ordinary children. And they loved it.

Living Books

What are "living books" which form a part of the daily nutrition proper for a child?

We should be deeply thankful that we live at a time when there is such a wealth of books available in the English language. It is a great responsibility to choose books, whether for home, school curriculum, or church. One must again remember that education does not happen only at school. The family, in fact, may be the only source of true education available to some children. At school they may well not be given any imaginative mind-food at all. Or, conversely, it may be the child's home that never feeds the mind. That child's needs must be met in other places, such as school or church.

The short selection which follows is of books which our own family has enjoyed together. If one were considering a curriculum, one would have to have a formal, comprehensive list covering all the necessary subjects. But these are some of our family's "living books"; they only serve as personal examples.

The Bible
Pilgrim Progress by John Bunyan
Tanglewood Tales by Nathaniel Hawthorne

The Chronicles of Narnia series by C. S. Lewis

Hans Christian Anderson's fairy tales

The Brothers Grimm's fairy tales

Peter Rabbit and other books by Beatrix Potter

Just So Stories by Rudyard Kipling

Little House on the Prairie series by Laura Ingalls Wilder

The Secret Garden by Frances Burnett

Abraham Lincoln by Ingrid and Edgar D'Aulaire

The Wind in the Willows by Kenneth Grahame

Johnny Tremaine by Esther Forbes

Carry on, Mr. Bowditch by Jean Lee Latham

Jane Eyre by Charlotte Bronte

Kon-Tiki by Thor Heyerdahl

Oliver Twist and *Hard Times* by Charles Dickens

William Shakespeare's plays—read aloud as plays, for shared
  pleasure. Try *The Merchant of Venice* and *Twelfth Night*

Robert Frost's poetry

The Oxford Book of English Verse

The Wheel on the School, The House of 60 Fathers, and other books
  by Meindert Dejong

The Heroes of Asgard by A. and E. Keary

The Silver Sword by Ian Serraillier

The Sheldon Book of Verses

A Wrinkle in Time and other books by Madeleine L'Engle

Ring Out Bow Bells by Cynthia Harnett

The Princess and the Goblin and other books by George MacDonald

The Lord of the Rings by J. R. R. Tolkien

And special mention goes to the Christian stories beloved now for
two generations:

Star of Light, Tanglewood Secrets, Treasures of the Snow,
and *Rainbow Garden* by Patricia St. John[12]

"Education," said Lord Haldane, some time ago, "is a matter of the spirit"—no wiser word has been said on the subject, and yet we persist in applying education from without as a bodily activity or emollient. We begin to see light. No one knoweth the things of man but the spirit of a man which is in him; therefore, there is no education but self-education and as soon as a young child begins his education he does so as a student. Our business is to give him mind-stuff, and both quality and quantity are essential. Naturally, each of us possesses this mind-stuff only in limited measure, but we know where to procure it; for the best thought the world possesses is stored in books; we must open books to children, the best books; our own concern is abundant and orderly serving.

I am jealous for the children; every modern educational movement tends to belittle them intellectually; and no-one more so than a late ingenious attempt to feed normal children with the pap-meat which may (?) be good for the mentally sick.[13]

Let me try to indicate some of the advantages of the theory I am urging:—It fits all ages, even the seven ages of man! It satisfies brilliant children and discovers intelligence in the dull. It secures attention, interest, concentration, without effort on the part of the teacher or the taught.

Children, I think, all children, so taught express themselves in forcible and fluent English and use a copious vocabulary. . . . Over thirty years ago . . . it occurred to me that a series of curricula might be devised embodying sound principles and securing that children should be in a position of less dependence on their teacher than they were; in other words, that their education should be largely self-education. A sort of correspondence school was set up [the PNEU School], the motto of which—"I am, I can, I ought, I will," has had much effect in throwing children upon the possibilities, capabilities, duties and determining power belonging to them as persons.[14]

The self-education begins with *listening* to carefully chosen books read out loud to the child every day. He then sometimes tells back in his own words what he has heard. Or he may draw a picture to illustrate what he has pictured in his imagination. When older, the same child will *read* for himself and *write* essays which narrate some part of what he has read.

The young child of six will spend twenty minutes a day—or whatever is practical—learning the mechanics of reading and writing. All children are different; there is no "normal" age when the child is "ready." And the speed of mastery will vary enormously. This process should be carried out in a friendly, quiet, regular, and structured way. A child should never be made to feel that he is lagging behind others of his age. We don't harass babies of eighteen months to walk if they still crawl. Einstein only started talking at four years!

By being allowed to learn at their own speed, the children taught by Charlotte Mason were happy with their mastery of skills. They did not "fail" or "pass." They learned how to read and write accurately. A high standard was expected, but at a level appropriate to the child's ability. It was like climbing one's own private ladder. It was *not* to be like a race.

"Good little Sally made only one mistake, she gets an A!" But poor struggling Johnny tried his best and is rewarded with a D.

How can Johnny ever take a proper joy in the fact that he learned a new step? When one three-year-old in the family learned to ride a bike, we all clapped and smiled. Another time, another child with quite different gifts learned to ride a two-wheeler at six years. Such smiles! He was as pleased as punch with himself. And that was as it should be.

The Bible teaches that we are like parts of a body. In other words, we are different from each other, we all have different gifts. How immoral to apply an arbitrary yardstick to the little child and expect him to progress at some "normal" speed! We take from him the joy of accomplishing new skills which should be part of growing up.

We often combine frustrating skill-learning techniques with sawdust books. Try instead this other, Christian approach. Expect high standards, but let them be appropriate to the individual who is progressing at his own rate of development. Make the lesson a short one, so that inattention does not become a habit. Follow the "skill lessons" with a varied diet of mind-food.

For example, when you read at home to children, you are sharing the interest of a short gospel story, followed by, say, a chapter of *The Lion, the Witch and the Wardrobe*.

There is no question of failing or passing. Instead there is joy. Afterward, if the child tells you the story back, you might comment, "That was especially good tonight. I like the way you described the woods."

Excellence is a *habit*. One four-year-old's level of attainment may fully equal that of another eight-year-old. That does not mean that the eight-year-old is inferior. Both may be excellent in their work, attention, and effort.

All children should have an excellent diet of mind-food to be nurtured on, so that their true education can begin. All children deserve great care in the building skills of literacy and numeracy, to build a foundation upon which they can carry on their own education at a later stage.

Let us apply this principle to the actual detailed practice in schools or homes.

A seven-year-old happens to need a short period of phonic practice, followed by reading a story out loud to you haltingly every day. He then laboriously concentrates on learning the mechanics of writing for ten to fifteen minutes. This does not mean to say that his mind should be left "frozen" at the level of his skills. When the essential, regular practice has been completed, the child puts all his little books and papers away, and turns his full attention to the adult. She will now be the medium through which he can "read" *real* books (not second-rate books).

Perhaps she reads a short portion from *Pilgrim's Progress*. She must, of course, be a person who wants to understand and enjoy this herself. When she has finished, the children might tell back the story, or act out the episode in play. They could make a scroll, as our children did in their PNEU school. As the pilgrim proceeds through various experiences, the children draw pictures of what they remember of the story. They end with the knowledge that life is a pilgrimage. They hear about the River at the end. (By the way, this is the only book that the PNEU recommended to be slightly abridged.)

Pilgrim's Progress will be read perhaps twice a week. After this, the children's next lesson might be a chapter of a well-written biography of a historical figure. Again the children listen with interest and build up knowledge. And so one proceeds. Science books will not be written in "second-grade language." Choose an interesting book that really explains things in lively language. Perhaps you will start with one on the animals and plants the child can see in his environment. Again, you read a short while. The children respond with a narration. You stop before they become restless.

The morning's program is intense, interesting but fairly short. It finishes early, leaving the child free to relax and "be."

By the time such educated children are nine or ten they will, of course, have been reading for themselves a long time. They will be ready to read a Shakespeare play (more of that later). They will enjoy and understand a really rich diet of books, essays, letters, plays, and poetry. They will have thought, discussed, and shared these ideas along with their own personal ideas.

Is this idealistic? Does it work? The answer is, yes. I had a child of six, Kirsteen, in a bright little school. She was happy enough, and learned to read and write after a fashion. There were hamsters, plants, paints, and lots of little booklets. There were special TV programs, the cute sort that are intended to grab the child's attention. When she came home, she sometimes talked about something that had happened. But there wasn't much to discuss.

Kirsteen's older sister, Margaret, was faring worse, at ages nine and ten. She was frustrated, had a low opinion of her own achievements, and had no interest in education.

One January day, God opened a door for them into a school where *true* education was going on. This was a small PNEU school, run in a classroom built onto the back of someone's private home, looking into an English country garden.

After the first day, Kirsteen came home glowing with life and interest. "We had the most *exciting* story today, but Mrs. Norton stopped at just the wrong place. I can't *wait* to hear the next part of the story!" And what was this exciting, vitalizing story? To my astonishment, it was *Pilgrim's Progress*, read to them in the original.

The quite electrifying change in those two children is really indescribable. They had so much to talk about! A wealth of literature, history, art, which was so glorious to work through. Their eyes became brighter, their minds alert. We had grand discussions, again and again. Shakespeare became a friend whose writing was much loved. The children would argue about the actual characters; for instance, whether Hermione was right or wrong, and what the old shepherd was actually up to (they were enjoying *The Winter's Tale*). The children read, every Friday, part of a Shakespeare play, each taking a different part. This from age nine! Once a year they would act one of the plays in the garden. In this way, they would enjoy three Shakespeare plays a year. They loved it all so much.

Some people were incredulous. "It's not possible," they responded. "Children just aren't up to that."

But they are   if the door is opened. There is only one problem that I can see. The adult, whether teacher or parent, has to be able to enjoy and understand what he or she is reading with the children.

When a child myself, I once took my two-year-old brother to visit a poor elderly peasant woman in a hovel of a chalet in Switzerland. I chatted with her in French, but her eyes opened in disbelief as the young child conversed with me in lively English. She turned to me and said with awe, "Such a *young* child—and he has learned *English*! It is so *hard* to learn English. He must be a genius!"

The person rises to understand, master, and enjoy whatever he is surrounded with in language, ideas, literature, and in appreciation of beauty. If you share with children the very best, carefully chosen to meet their needs, they will amaze everyone.

I have heard of a fascinating confirmation of this principle. A television program which I did not myself see, but which several students at L'Abri described to me, showed the work of Marva

Collins, a black American woman who obviously had an educated love and understanding of excellent literature.[15] She became discouraged with the urban schools, which were damaging the children by classifying them as failures. She opened her own home as a school, and the neighborhood children were offered real education. The nation couldn't believe what they saw—ghetto children who were avidly "into" good books, who enjoyed Shakespeare as much as the little children far away in their PNEU school in Sussex. What a challenge! What a relief! There is no normal child who will not respond to proper feeding, either physically, spiritually, or mentally.

It is cheering that however miserable the environment, however many limitations there are to overcome or accept, the riches of good books may bring healing education. The light of new ideas and interest can be used anywhere and at any age for all persons. Books of merit are open doors to a lifetime of exploration.

A friend has been working in an inner-city junior high school in the USA. His students were classified as "remedial." In fact, the staff treated them as beyond educational help. However, a willing publishing industry churned out endless "remedial programs" that cost umpteen dollars to produce. The fact that these same children had been fruitlessly working with similar materials for eight years had not caused anybody to pause and reflect.

My friend took the "impossible" ones and closed the doors. The workbooks gathered dust, but in the quietness you could hear a pin drop. What's going on?

He is reading a really *good* book out loud. They're trapped, interested, wanting to know what happens next in the story. "Oh, no—the bell's rung. Why are we here such a *short* time?"

My friend also gave children help in learning to read themselves. He was rewarded. They were having discussions in class. The discussions stimulated thinking. ("They're sharp!" says my friend.) Later on, he found to his astonishment that those kids had been borrowing and reading those same books.

Charlotte Mason's ideas are especially needed by deprived children today, the ones who are bored. It is a challenge to *us* to keep alive the eagerness the nine-month-old child displays when a cupboard is left open. Life is just too interesting for boredom!

3

Authority and Freedom

Children: Good and Bad

Two of my friends were talking about their children. "They're such monsters," one announced, "that I dread it when I think of the vacation ahead. I'm sure I'll run out of punishments."

"Oh, mine are perfect darlings in themselves!" retorted the other. "I always think that children seem to bring a bit of heaven with them! It's *our* bad world that rubs off on them!"

Educators, psychologists, and theologians have all struggled with the same problem. Are children basically good creatures or evil creatures? Should we side with the "all freedom" brigade or the "beat it out of them" brigade?

Charlotte Mason's approach was friendly, reasonable, and realistic. She knew that the biblical teaching on this subject applies to each person regardless of age. We are all under God's authority. Although we all share in the fallen human condition, there is also the positive, good side of human nature.

The fact seems to be that children are like ourselves, not because they have to become so, but because they are born so; that is, with tendencies, dispositions, towards good and evil, and also with a curious intuitive knowledge as to which is good and which is evil. Here we have the work of education indicated. There are good and evil tendencies in body and mind, heart and soul; and the hope set before us is that we can foster the good so as to attenuate the evil; that is, on condition that we put education in her true place as the handmaid of Religion.[1]

The first task of education is a moral one, with the Judeo-Christian framework giving direction. In a fallen world, we would end up with hopelessness and depression if it were not for the glorious reality of God's revealed word.

We are not victims of despair, darkness, or the evil in ourselves or the world. There *is* righteousness, goodness, holiness, fairness, wholeness. This is an objective truth, the very substance of the infinite God who is indeed there and who has not been silent. And so we, the finite, can know. We don't have to search within our own selves to find the way. There is relief. We are sheep; we have been given a shepherd. We who sit in darkness have been given a great light.

As each of us *is* a sinner, and we fail to meet the standard of perfection required by God, we accept the beautiful, free, and generous gift of God, who gave his own Son.

And so Charlotte Mason asks:

But what sort of approaches do we prepare for children towards the God whom they need, the Saviour in Whom is all help, the King Who affords all delight, commands all adoration and loyalty? Any words or thoughts of ours are poor and insufficient, but we have a treasury of divine words which they read and know with satisfying pleasure and tell with singular beauty and fitness.[2]

The child should be given the source material on the subject of right and wrong directly from the Bible. And not in such quantities, or wrapped in such tangles of verbiage, that the mind switches off.

When a group of people sit together and read one biblical sentence, for example, "Be ye kind one to another" (Eph. 4:32 KJV), if we are honest, it pricks our hearts. The adult is as much under the authority of Scripture's laws as the child. In a sense, I do not teach this to the child, or to any other person who is ignorant of God's word. Instead, we share together his words which teach us all. And the Holy Spirit is the Person who then takes God's words and applies them to my own personal life at that moment.

This is deeply significant. As a parent, I hold an office under God. But I have no right to impose arbitrary rules upon those under me. We are *all* under God's authority. We are in the same boat. There is another important sense in which this is true. Although we enjoy the good in each child, he needs to be improved. He does wrong. He either ignores or chooses against that which he knows is right. *But so do I.*

This doesn't soften the law.

"Johnny, it is wrong to take that coin, it doesn't belong to you."

"Sally, you can't throw that heavy brick at Jane, however angry you feel."

But the reason why is not because *I* say so, but because it is actually *wrong*, right back to infinity. We march under the same orders. And it helps so much to have that honest and sympathetic remark, "I know it's hard. I feel like thumping people, too, sometimes." Or,

"I haven't been tempted to steal, but I know how hard it is to avoid doing something that I am tempted by. I've found it helps to . . ."

This does not change the fact that it is helpful to make sure that appropriate consequences follow a wrongdoing. "Sally, since you hurt Jane, you'll have to come inside and help clean the floor. You can't play right now." Sally will probably agree that she deserves to have her free time of playing outside removed. In the Bible, the result of wrongdoing was usually related to the offense. So, for instance, one who stole would not only have to pay back the original, but would have to work to give back several times its value. Children really respect this sort of fair consequence.

The basis of a wholesome approach to life with children is an appreciation of them as people, and at the same time a realistic understanding of how we are going to be doers of the Lord's word and not hearers only.

Charlotte Mason believed that the right habits should be established in childhood. If very small children are helped to do right in the course of their day, surely the habit of right-doing will help them later, when they face bigger and harder things. The first habit, of course, is obedience. In fact, this is the single greatest pattern to be formed.

It is wrong to choose an issue which goes across the natural grain and to make the child "obey" in a grim, unnatural way. A tired two-year-old may not go up to bed at the chosen time. Better to divert his attention and carry him up warmly held in your arms.

Drawing the line at actions likely to endanger the child—"Don't put that fork in the outlet," or "You can't play with the stove"— is necessary. But so, too, are positive acts such as, "Take time to listen to your grandmother. Don't run out when she is speaking," or "Treat the baby carefully," or "They are persons like you; they deserve respect and care." Children can be helped to acquire the habit of treating others as they should. This habit of respecting persons, thinking of them, and being polite is fostered when the child himself is used to consideration, time, and care. It is a two-way matter.

> Ninety-nine out of a hundred things we do, are done, well or ill, as mere matters of habit. . . . It is startling and shocking that there are many children of thoughtful parents whose lives are spent in day-long efforts of decision upon matters which it is their parents' business to settle for them. . . . Every point in the day's routine is discussed, nothing comes with the comforting ease of a matter of course; the child always prefers to do something else, and commonly does it. . . . Children are before all things reasonable beings, and to some children of acute and powerful intelligence, an arbitrary and apparently unreasonable command is cruelly irritating. It is not advisable to answer children categorically when they want to know the why for every command, but wise parents steer a middle course. They are careful to form habits upon which the routine of life runs easily and, when the exceptional event requires a new regulation they may make casual mention of their reasons for having so and so done; or, if this is not convenient and the case is a trying one, they give the children the reason for all obedience—"for this is right." In a word, authority avoids, so far as may be, giving cause of offence.[3]

Life at home and at school provides many areas in which helpful habits can be formed. Big moral efforts can then be saved for significant battles and choices and not be frittered away on issues such as bedtime or TV. A habitual routine is accepted, and many duties and attitudes are taken for granted.

As this framework is established, care must be taken that it suits the child at that particular stage. Physical, emotional, and developmental aspects must be provided for. For instance, have you ever seen an insistent adult wasting time trying to secure cooperation from a small child who should have had supper, a story, and bedtime at least an hour previously? We help children when we spend time on understanding them. Are two children forever fighting? Maybe it's because they come home exhausted. Could they be helped by having a cozy story, with the littlest one being given a cuddle on your lap, as soon as they come home? Nutrition can be given with wheat-germ muffins and milk. Bolstered by having this need met, they will surely be helped to live together in greater peace.

"Blessed are the peacemakers" (Matt. 5:9). I believe all adults who have an office of authority over children should meditate on this regularly. These questions about the application of God's moral laws require thoughtfulness, balance, and intuition. Love, common sense, and sensitivity to areas where freedom is necessary are needed. As a parent I find that I often need to rethink what I am doing and why. The following section from Charlotte Mason is so helpful that I will quote it at length, and then comment on some of the ways in which this wisdom is relevant and applicable today.

We need not add that authority is just and faithful in all matters of promise-keeping; it is also considerate, and that is why a good mother is the best home-ruler; she is in touch with the children, knows their unspoken schemes and half-formed desires, and where she cannot yield, she diverts; she does not crush with a sledgehammer, an instrument of rule with which a child is somehow never very sympathetic. . . . We all know how important this is, of changing children's thoughts, diverting, in the formation of habit. Let us not despise the day of small things nor grow weary in well-doing; if we have trained our children from their earliest years to prompt mechanical obedience, well and good; we reap our reward. If we have not, we must be content to lead by small degrees, by ever-watchful efforts, by authority never in abeyance and never aggressive, to "the joy of self-control," the delight of proud chivalric obedience which will hail a command as an opportunity for service. It is a happy thing that the "difficult" children who are the readiest to resist a direct command are often the quickest to respond to the stimulus of an idea. . . . I am not proposing a one-sided arrangement, all the authority on the one part and all the docility on the other; for never was there a child who did not wield authority, if only over dolls or tin soldiers. . . . Authority is that aspect of love which parents present to their children; parents know that it is love, because to them it means continual self-denial, self-repression, self-sacrifice; children recognize it as love, because to them it means quiet rest and gaiety of heart. Perhaps the best aid to the maintenance of authority in the home is for those in authority to ask themselves daily that question which was presumptuously put to our Lord— "Who gave Thee this authority?"[4]

Authority: A Balance

Consideration

Now that we have reached the last quarter of the twentieth century, the greatest priority for many seems to be, *Do the best for me and myself. My needs, my career—I come first.* This is such a prevalent view that Christians are also liable to be drawn into the attitude of believing that we don't need to sacrifice the time and effort that serving others demands. One of the saddest results is legalistic parents who tell their children what to do but forget what loving them means. The time, kindness, support, and consideration needed to serve a child are considerable.

Consideration begins with—

UNDERSTANDING THE CHILD'S NEEDS

Charlotte Mason states that a mother is the most likely person to truly understand her children. I think that she would have been delighted with one modern trend: the many fathers who have so ordered their lives that they, too, develop a deep affinity with their children. What richness when both the mother and the father have this living friendly relationship! Although mothers and fathers can both only reflect imperfectly the great parenting-in-love of our Heavenly Father, it is still good.

Teachers and schools are often pressed with curriculum and/or examination requirements, the aim being to mesh children into our society like so many cogs in a wheel. They must here take heed if they are to put into practice Christian principles. They should appreciate the nuances of the individual child and seek to *serve the child*, not the system.

This is an area where direct relationships teach more than endless textbooks, courses, or theories. Respect, watch, learn, love.

Sadly, our fast-moving generation is often so involved in the rat race that this gentle art of understanding, appreciating, and loving the child never has a chance to be practiced by mother, father, or anyone else. We have to set our priorities straight. Can we serve God's lambs wholeheartedly while we are being consumed with career demands? When there is no parent who makes it his business to understand the individual child, and the people whose job it is to care for him treat him as part of *their* careers, perhaps the only place where that child will find understanding is in the counselor's office for one hour a week.

The Christian community is confronted by countless children whose parents do not fulfill their duty and privilege. It is *our* duty then, under God, to try to provide that considerate and loving authority which the child is lacking. We may not be able to provide a perfect substitute for the ideal of a caring family, but that shouldn't stop us from doing *something*. Remember that even one stumbling-block removed from a child's path counts.

Justice

Authority must be based on true righteousness. We in authority look to the Bible for direction. It has to be fair. We must base our requirements upon what is right. We should watch out so as not to add extra burdens which will clutter up a child's life. However, part of what is right and just is that the child should learn to accept the small duties and habits necessary for living together. Therefore it is "just" to be polite, to come for meals when they are ready, and to share in the necessary chores. The areas which are "just" include these small practical areas, and in fact, help one to the acceptance of the bigger commitments. But to be just, we have to respect the person's individuality, just as God respects us.

Faithfulness

Faithfulness means consistency. The child knows he can depend on you. The adult in authority is faithful to the child; how else can we expect him to learn to be faithful to *his* duties?

"Does not crush," said Charlotte Mason, ". . . leads." The shepherd doesn't smash his lambs. The pasture itself is a discipline, for it has boundaries. But in the pasture, there is freedom to move, and needs are met. The reality of righteousness is a clear hard line. We should daily look into God's word and see this path by his clear light. The shepherd leads into the paths of righteousness.

Imagine a frustrated adult, at home or school, shouting, "Tom, you never try *hard*. You don't care. I knew you wouldn't bother to listen."

Contrast this with a leader who knows that Tom's problem is that he is getting into the habit of doing things poorly and not bothering to listen. He takes the responsibility of helping to lead Tom into better habits. Perhaps he will say, "Tom, come over here where it is quieter." The adult may lift Tom onto his lap, if little, or sit down next to the older child. He knows that Tom needs to change. The tone is friendly and expects cooperation; it's positive and cheerful. "Tom, yesterday when I asked you to finish that job, you just walked off after five minutes. That isn't going to work, and I'm not going to let you get into the habit of doing that. I know that you can try really hard when you choose to. I'd like to see a carefully finished job today. I know that you really can do it because . . . [here he will refer to a specific example of an appropriate accomplishment] . . . Now you sit here, where it is quieter, and finish this job. How long do you think it'll take?"

The leader hasn't let Tom get away. He is *leading* him in small steps. When Tom can feel satisfied with accomplishing a set task with regularity, new habits of success will begin to be established. Tom will switch off even more completely if the verbal sledgehammer of total judgment from above cries, "You are hopeless, you don't try, etc." This is *not* offering help or leadership. When human beings, at any age, are *expected* to do badly, it is too easy to become discouraged, accept the judgment, and live down to it.

In England, when the top 15 percent used to be creamed off and sent to top "academic" schools, one headmaster (principal) conducted a small private experiment. He took a few children, whose test results had actually placed them well below that top group. Without telling his staff, he put them into the elite classes.

Of course, the children and teachers assumed that the tests had projected what sort of person they were—clever and capable. And those youngsters lived up to what the situation told them they could achieve.

Of course, this wouldn't work in every instance. But what a truth it demonstrates! Assume and tell a child again and again that he is bad, selfish, or lazy, and you will bind him by your expectations. If you expect what is good, and are not shocked by the reality of the faltering footsteps toward it, you will be well on the way to leading. If you can be positive, friendly, and helpful in building the right patterns, many of the vexed authority questions will fall into place.

Diversion

Charlotte Mason believed this was an essential policy, both for the adult leading the young child, and for ourselves when we practice self-discipline at any age. If you see a situation looming up where the child's weakness will probably result in error, it is better to divert the child. For a tiny child, this may mean suggesting some delightful activity so that their thoughts are diverted from the wrongdoing that they were about to engage in.

You see fiery-tempered Jane pick up a stick and look angrily at her foe. Perhaps you can come to her in a friendly way saying, "Put the stick down, Jane. Could you please help me get popcorn for everybody?" If that is something Jane really likes doing, your suggestion will have the desired effect.

Later on, it is a great help to be taught this way of helping ourselves in our weaknesses to do what is right. Suppose I was an alcoholic, and I had wrestled and won a hard fight with myself and my tendencies. It would be helpful to be aware that I shouldn't trust myself with too much temptation. Therefore, if I were facing a long air flight, and I used to drink at such times, I would help to divert myself by buying a book I'd been longing to read.

After all, we are attempting to help the child so that sooner, rather than later, he will have a mature *self-control* under God's law.

We help a child in this lifelong struggle if we love him and like him. True appreciation will help give the child the lifelong strength of not having to struggle for a proper self-respect. All teachers know that the most "unteachable" children are those who have lost self-confidence. They don't think much of themselves; they too easily sit down in despair under the labels which describe and limit them. Is it strange that everything seems to come back to love and moral framework? If we have truly understood reality, we realize that this is the touchstone of the matter. God is *love*, and He is *perfectly holy*.

Authority Never in Abeyance

God's law stands at all times. And the Lord God of Israel's loving care never takes a vacation. "Indeed, he . . . will neither slumber nor sleep"(Ps. 121:4).

This doesn't mean I have to continually hover anxiously over the child. It is necessary that children should have room and time to play without a watchful eye judging their every move. How else can they mature? It is wonderful for children to be able to be trusted. But it should always be freedom within known limits, both physically and morally.

But—and I see this as a really big "But"—with all the families rushing about to jobs and endless activities, many children today have "authority in abeyance." I believe, as did Charlotte Mason, that children's freedom should be surrounded by adults who bear the final responsibility for what is happening. Maybe your six-year-old has played for six hours at "camping" with his friends, out under some trees. Maybe they were quite independent all that time. This is good. But it is also necessary that a caring adult knows what is going on. They are independent, yes, but with the freedom of being in a pasture, not the danger of hiking alone through the mountaintops. No responsible leader lets a child get into the physical and moral danger of being quite alone.

Authority Never Aggressive

When I am honest, as a parent, I know that I am all too often aggressive toward the child. I am angry at him because I am angry at my own failures. I want this child to be the perfect human being that I somehow failed to become. It is shockingly easy to take my frustrations out on those who are under me. This is a matter of humility. My child respects me better when I come to him saying, "I'm sorry I shouted at you. I'm really worried and exhausted tonight, and I took it out on you. You should have remembered to put your muddy boots away, but my reaction was wrong." Or simply, "I'm sorry. I'm wrong."

None of us live up very well to that model of righteousness, the loving Shepherd-Leader who is perfect Himself and can lead into the paths of righteousness in love.

Such honesty strengthens our office. For we are only pointing in some poor way *toward* what is good. Thank God that the reality of righteousness is not based on the level I achieve myself! We look to Jesus, the author and finisher of our faith. What shall I do when Tom doesn't finish a reasonable and clearly explained job in ten minutes, or when Jane carries on and hits her foe?

Certain consequences can be made to fit the omission or commission. The job may have to be finished in playtime. Jane may have to leave the game she is playing.

Charlotte Mason does not go deeply into the issue of corporal punishment. This is, I believe, because she gave principles and guiding lines. After this, the individual in authority has the responsibility of choosing an appropriate method. A sharp quick smack on a toddler's hand, for example, delivered with the purpose of stopping him from playing with the stove, along with a firm "No" and the physical removal from the danger area, works well.

Some parents (including ourselves) have found that the time-honored spanking draws the final line clearly and without argument for young children. But it is not the only way, and one must be wary of violence and anger. As a parent, I personally would not be happy to entrust the walking of this delicate line to a nonparent.

Charlotte Mason felt that teacher or parent could successfully enforce the "lines" without using any form of physical punishment.

She knew that the *basis* for authority (which is the actual existence of a final morality) gives a sure stability from which to act. This sureness gives all of us, as human beings, a stability, as we know that it is right to follow the rules laid down by our Creator. Because we are certain of what is right, we know that we and the children must walk this path. Harshness, fear, and autocracy are ruled out if we follow the New Testament teaching that leadership means a *serving* of the other person. The child is respected, his needs and abilities are considered, and he is lifted up. We are to lead in love. We can ponder what this means (perhaps weekly!) by reading 1 Corinthians 13:1–13.

In my experience, children obey best when their lives are as fully satisfying as possible in the way Charlotte Mason advocated. If minds are interested; skills are being learned; loving relationships are enjoyed; creativity is encouraged; beauty in nature, art, and music are appreciated; hours are spent in free play; and children learn to climb, swim, ride, canoe, ski, or skate—why, these children will be well on the way to having their sinful natures put in the back seat! Sinful natures expand like a malignancy at any age with loneliness, mental poverty, boredom, passivity, hunger, tiredness, and deprivation of daily contact with the rich source material of goodness—the word of God. When you think about it, many children today have hell on earth. Are we surprised at what happens?

But if we make life so rich, won't our children flounder when they hit reality? The Bible indicates that if we grow in love, if our minds are established in knowledge, if we know that we are secure, if we know something of goodness, we will be all the stronger for the fight ahead. "Whatever is true, whatever is noble, whatever is right, whatever is pure, whatever is lovely, whatever is admirable—if anything is excellent or praiseworthy—think about such things" (Phil. 4:8). Real life brings hardship, disappointments, the reality of sin. One reason why Charlotte Mason contrasted the organized, child-centered atmosphere of the pleasant kindergarten (which she described as *too smooth* for the child), with the home was the reality possible in a home situation. In the kindergarten, on the other hand,

Everything is directed, expected, suggested. No other personality out of book, picture, or song, no, not even that of Nature herself, can get at the children without the mediation of the teacher. No room is left for spontaneity or personal initiation on their part. . . . Most of us are misled by our virtues, and the entire zeal and enthusiasm of the teacher is perhaps her stone of stumbling. "But the children are so happy and good!" Precisely: the home-nursery is by no means such a scene of peace, but I venture to think it a better growing-place.[5]

Understood Boundaries

Why a better growing-place, morally as well as in other ways? Charlotte Mason has both feet firmly on the ground. Not for her the greenhouse atmosphere where sturdy personalities are shielded from their own awkwardness, failure, and the stark reality of life not in an artificial environment. On the one hand, we are to help the child to form good habits. But on the other hand, at home it is easier to give him freedom to make mistakes and bear the consequences. A huge magnifying glass need not be used to scrutinize the uncomfortable child. He need not be talked at and guided self-consciously. There should be relaxed normality in which to live, make mistakes, brush off the dust, and carry on without too much fuss.

What a challenge to read,

. . . the principle of obedience is within him [the child] waiting to be called into existence. There is no need to berate the child, or threaten him, or use any manner of violence, because the parent is *invested* with authority which the child intuitively recognises. It is enough to say, 'Do this,' in a quiet authoritative tone, and *expect it to be done.* The mother often loses her hold over her children because they detect in the tone of her voice that she does not expect them to obey her behests; she does not think enough of her position; has not sufficient confidence in her own authority. The mother's great stronghold is in the habit of obedience.[6]

Charlotte Mason goes on:

Tardy, unwilling, occasional obedience is hardly worth the having; and it is greatly easier to give the child the habit of perfect obedience by never allowing him anything else, than it is to obtain this mere formal obedience by a constant exercise of authority. By-and-by, when he is old enough, *take the child into confidence* (you are on his side); let him know what a noble thing it is to be able to make himself do, in a minute, and brightly, the very thing he would rather not do. To secure this habit of obedience, the mother must exercise *great self-restraint* [temptation to use this for convenience]; she must never give a command which *she does not intend to see carried out to the full. And she must not lay upon her children burdens, grievous to be borne, of command heaped upon command.*

Children who are trained to perfect obedience may be trusted with a good deal of liberty: they receive a few directions which they know they must not disobey; and for the rest, they are left to learn how to direct their own actions, even at the cost of some small mishaps; and are not pestered with a perpetual fire of "Do this" and "Don't do that!"[7]

Ah, blessed balance! The few reasonable lines, firmly laid down, and then freedom within the pasture. Note especially, the importance of:

1. *Taking the child into confidence.* You are on *his* side. You are together aiming for the strength and maturity of character

which will help him, later on, cheerfully to be able to do what is right, rather than what is merely wanted. You discuss it together. You are allies on the path.

2. The parent has to *exercise great self-restraint.* It is easy to keep giving extra orders, loading up the child and turning him into an obedience-robot. We must show that we are mature enough to stick to the lines which are right, and that we don't merely boss the child about for our convenience. Furthermore, we must only give commands that we truly intend to see carried out to the full. This last is probably more powerful than spankings and punishments. The child knows the finality of the understood boundaries.

Parents should seek, prayerfully, to become worthy leaders with understanding, wisdom, and love. They should also consider very carefully whether a particular institution—be it school, camp, or other—will be the right place for their child. Children are able to understand that there *are* many people who do not believe in the framework of God's morality. We do them no favor if we shield them from the generation in which they must live. But we must tread with extreme care when we hand over to others the delicate task of providing for large chunks of the growing time of our children.

The slave-camp, sledgehammer, or mechanical approach is out, so far as I can see. Equally, a fully permissive no-base and do-as-you-feel atmosphere cannot lead to proper development. We must not legislate a final answer for each other. Some will find the most human and healthy school environment in the secular world, even though they see the limitations. They will fill in the groundwork at home. For others, conditions will be so inhuman or out of touch with the *true* reality of a moral framework that they will choose to provide a school or home education based on a Christian world-view. But this, to be healthy, can't be just a reaction to the secular culture. There is a danger of being imbalanced if we base our ideas of discipline, etc., on a reaction to any culture which is based on wrong thinking. Instead, balance comes through being positive and realistic. We have to study the child's needs as a person, and consider what is fully human, balanced, and whole. We need to juggle complicated pieces of a puzzle—the child, the community you live in, what is available, and what are the alternatives.

"If any of you lacks wisdom, he should ask God, who gives generously to all men without finding fault, and it will be given to him" (James 1:5).

4

A New Perspective

WE HAVE LOOKED at a few areas of Charlotte Mason's teaching, examining quotations from several of her books. Now I would like to go back over some of that ground, for it is impossible to consider every aspect at once. It is as if, walking through a forest, we cannot see for the trees. We climb a small hill and see the lay of the land. However, the next hillock offers a slightly different view, and we are able to guide our footsteps more knowingly as we take in a new perspective.

Early experiences often shape understanding. Charlotte Mason's first professional work stripped her of many previous assumptions. It is fascinating to join her and see the beginnings of her search for true education.

I had at the time just begun to teach, and was young and enthusi-astic in my work. It was to my mind a great thing to be a teacher; it was impossible but that a teacher should leave his stamp on the children. His own was the fault if anything went wrong, if any child did badly in school or out of it. There was no degree of responsibility to which youthful ardour was not equal. But, all this zeal notwithstanding, the disappointing thing was, that nothing extraordinary happened. The children were good on the whole, because they were the children of parents who had themselves been brought up with some care; but it was plain that they behaved very much as "'twas their nature to." The faults they had, they kept; the virtues they had were exercised just as fitfully as before. The good, meek little girl still told fibs. The bright, generous child was incurably idle. In lessons it was the same thing; the dawdling child went on dawdling, the dull child became no brighter. It was very disappointing. The children, no doubt, "got on"—a little; but each one of them had the makings in her of a noble character, of a fine mind, and where was the lever to lift each of these little worlds? Such a lever there must be. This horse-in-a-mill round of geography and French, history and sums, was no more than playing at education; for who remembers the scraps of knowledge he laboured over as a child? and would not the application of a few hours in later life effect more than a year's drudgery at any one subject in childhood? If education is to secure the step-by-step progress of the individual and the nation, it must mean something over and above the daily plodding at small tasks which goes by the name.

Looking for guidance to the literature of education, I learned much from various sources, though I failed to find what seemed to me an authoritative guide, that is, one whose thought embraced the possibilities contained in the human nature of a child, and, at the same time, measured the scope of education. I saw how religious teaching helped the children, gave them power and motives for continuous effort, and raised their desires towards the best things. I saw how law restrained from evil, and love impelled towards good. But with these great aids from without and from above, there was still the depressing sense of labouring at education in the dark; the advance made by the young people in moral, and even in intellectual power was like that of a door on its hinges—a swing forward today and back again tomorrow, with little sensible progress from year to year beyond that of being able to do harder sums and read harder books.

Consideration made the reason of the failure plain; there was a warm glow of goodness at the heart of every one of the children, but they were all incapable of steady effort, because they had no strength of will, no power to make themselves do that which they knew they ought to do. Here, no doubt, come in the functions of the parents and teachers; they should be able to make the child do that which he lacks the power to compel himself to do. But it were poor training that should keep the child dependent upon personal influence. It is the business of education to find some way of supplementing that weakness of will which is the bane of most of us as of the children.[1]

Read the above passage again in the light of your own experience. Have we come any further? Dare we be honest? How do we truly educate ourselves, as well as the child? Do we enjoy a rich, lifelong memory of the actual "education"?

The following "short synopsis" of the educational philosophy advanced by Charlotte Mason serves as our plan to establish a better educational practice than the "disappointing" experience of much school "education."[2]

1. Children are born persons.

2. They are not born either good or bad, but with possibilities for good and evil.

3. The principles of authority on the one hand and obedience on the other, are natural, necessary and fundamental; but—

4. These principles are limited by the respect due to the personality of children, which must not be encroached upon, whether by fear or love, suggestion or influence, or undue play upon any one natural desire.

5. Therefore we are limited to three educational instruments— the atmosphere of environment, the discipline of habit, and the presentation of living ideas.

6. By the saying, *Education is an atmosphere*, it is not meant that a child should be isolated in what may be called a "child environment," especially adapted and prepared; but that we should take into account the educational value of his natural home atmosphere, both as regards persons and things, and should let him live freely among his proper conditions. It stultifies a child to bring down his world to the "child's" level.

7. By *Education is a discipline*, is meant the discipline of habits formed definitely and thoughtfully, whether habits of mind or body. Physiologists tell us of the adaptation of brain structure to habitual lines of thought—i.e., to our habits.

8. In the saying that *Education is a life*, the need of intellectual and moral as well as of physical sustenance is implied. The mind feeds on ideas, and therefore children should have a generous curriculum.

9. But the mind is not a receptacle into which ideas must be dropped, each idea adding to an "apperception mass" of its like, the theory upon which the Herbartian doctrine of interest rests.

10. On the contrary, a child's mind is no mere *sac* to hold ideas; but is rather, if the figure may be allowed, a spiritual *organism*, with an appetite for all knowledge. This is its proper diet, with which it is prepared to deal, and which it can digest and assimilate as the body does foodstuffs.

11. This difference is not a verbal quibble. The Herbartian doctrine lays the stress of education—the preparation of knowledge in enticing morsels, presented in due order—upon the teacher. Children taught upon this principle are in danger of receiving much teaching with little knowledge; and the teacher's axiom is, "What a child learns matters less than how he learns it."

12. But, believing that the normal child has powers of mind that fit him, we must give him a full and generous curriculum; taking care, only, that the knowledge offered to him is vital—that is, that facts are not presented without their informing ideas. Out of this conception comes the principle that—

13. *Education is the science of relations*; that is, that a child has natural relations with a vast number of things and thoughts: so we must train him upon physical exercises, nature, handicrafts, science and art, and upon *many living* books; for we know that our business is, not to teach him all about anything, but to help him to make valid as many as may be of—

"Those first-born affinities
That fit our new existence to existing things."

14. There are also two secrets of moral and intellectual self-management which should be offered to children; these we may call the Way of the Will and the Way of the Reason.

15. *The Way of the Will.*—Children should be taught—

(a) To distinguish between "I want" and "I will."
(b) That the way to will effectively is to turn our thoughts from that which we desire but do not will.
(c) That the best way to turn our thoughts is to think of or do some quite different thing, entertaining or interesting.
(d) That, after a little rest in this way, the will returns to its work with new vigour.

(This adjunct of the will is familiar to us as *diversion*, whose office it is to ease us for a time from will effort, that we may "will" again with added power. The use of suggestion—even self-suggestion—as an aid to the will, is to be deprecated, as tending to stultify and stereotype character. It would seem that spontaneity is a condition of development, and that human nature needs the discipline of failure as well as of success.)

16. *The Way of the Reason.*—We should teach children, too, not to "lean" (too confidently) "unto their own understanding," because the function of reason is, to give logical demonstration (a) of mathematical truth; and (b) of an initial idea, accepted by the will. In the former case reason is, perhaps, an infallible

guide, but in the second it is not always a safe one; for whether that initial idea be right or wrong, reason will confirm it by irrefragable proofs.

17. Therefore children should be taught, as they become mature enough to understand such teaching, that the chief responsibility which rests on them as persons is the acceptance or rejection of initial ideas. To help them in this choice we should give them principles of conduct and a wide range of the knowledge fitted for them.

These three principles (15, 16 and 17) should save children from some of the loose thinking and heedless action which cause most of us to live at a lower level than we need.

18. We should allow no separation to grow up between the intellectual and "spiritual" life of children; but should teach them that the divine Spirit has constant access to their spirits, and is their continual helper in all the interests, duties and joys of life.[3]

We will use this outline and approach as the basic framework of the next part of this book: each element deserves close examination. You'll notice that I've already expanded the first three points in the previous chapters, so we can go straight to point four, which states:

These principles are limited by the respect due to the personality of children, which must not be encroached upon, whether by fear or love, suggestion or influence, or undue play upon any one natural desire.

The presuppositions on which this statement is based are completely different from the usual non-Christian assumptions of today.

The normal secular worldview today is, by definition, non-Christian. The "person" is not sacred, nor is he revered, respected, or worth anything on his own. There isn't an objective structure, and the finality of death without the Christian hope removes ultimate perspectives.

Against this, the Christian believes that there is truth, as revealed to us by God in his word, the Bible. We know that he is the final authority; he has personality (he is Triune). We therefore have a philosophical explanation for the experience of the human personality. It is no fluke. It is real: morality, free choice, ideas, love, creativity. We have duties, responsibilities, aims, and joys. We have value. In education, the resulting principles and practice will be quite different from those based on a totally different view of man and reality. As my dad, Francis Schaeffer, says in his book *A Christian Manifesto*:

> They (the Huxleys) understood . . . that they would bring forth two totally different conclusions, both for the individuals and for society. What we must understand is that the two worldviews really do bring forth with inevitable certainty not only personal differences, but also total differences in regard to society, government, and law.
>
> There is no way to mix these two worldviews. They are separate entities that cannot be synthesized.[4]

One of the areas deeply affected by the "totally different" view is education. This includes society, government, and law—both in the day-by-day life of the child and the ultimate aim of his education. In other words, the "philosophy of education."

I state this as relevant to the fourth of Charlotte Mason's considerations. The Christian view of the child does not allow him to be conditioned as a dog may be conditioned to respond to a bell. We must have due respect for the sacredness of his separate personality. Therefore, we treat him with dignity, allowing for his weakness and need of support at any given stage.

We saw that Charlotte Mason accepted the practicality of God's moral law being the guide to all human action. There is no wavering here. For instance, it is not only wrong to steal; it is also wrong to disobey those with proper authority over us.

However, Charlotte Mason felt that this should not be obtained by methods which encroach on the personality of children. A child whose life is shaped by fear does not share the sweet joy of the lamb scampering in the shepherd's pasture. Therefore, the child is not to be forced to "do his duty" (be it learning a times table or remembering to put muddy boots away) because if he doesn't all hell will be let loose on him. Nor should he be enticed to do so because, "It makes me so happy if you do." He should like and love those who are responsible for his child-life. But he isn't just to do things to make somebody he cares about happy. One day you won't be there to see! No, he must learn that he does it because it is *right*.

Charlotte Mason says:

For the action of fear as a governing motive we cannot do better than read again our *David Copperfield* (a great educational treatise) and study "Mr. Creakle" in detail for terrorism in the schoolroom and "Mr. Murdstone" for the same vice in the home.[5]

This needs emphasizing, as there are those who have reacted to permissiveness by a swing to harsh discipline, sometimes even fear and terrorism. Reactions are dangerous. This can also bring the sledgehammer type of discipline which we have already discussed. But note that fear is not the only emotion that can be wrongly used to manipulate the child (or any person).

Charlotte Mason goes on to say,

We have methods more subtle than the mere terrors of the law. Love is one of these. The person of winning personality attracts his pupils who will do anything for his sake and are fond and eager in all their ways, docile to the point where personality is submerged, and they live on the smiles, perish on the averted looks, of the adored teacher. Parents look on with a smile and think that all is well; but Bob or Mary is losing that growing time which should make a self-dependent, self-ordered person, and is day by day becoming a parasite who can go only as he is carried, the easy prey of fanatic or demagogue. This sort of encroach-ment upon the love of children offers as a motive, "do this for my sake"; wrong is to be avoided lest it grieve the teacher, good is to be done to pleasure him; for this end a boy learns his lessons, behaves properly, shows good will, produces a whole catalogue of schoolboy virtues and yet his character is being undermined.[6]

Charlotte Mason goes on to explain that if one uses suggestion and personal influence to manipulate boys and girls, they do not learn to stand on their own two feet in reference to an outside ob-jective moral standard. One of the greatest dangers of strong adults is that they can encourage children to be weak or even parasites. We, each one, whatever our age, intelligence, or sex, have the responsibility of acting within the definite framework given in God's word. Since Jesus Christ's earthly work, nobody is to act as a priest for anybody. And the Holy Spirit is the one who works deeply into our personal lives. We must never presume to usurp his work. It is dangerous to think that we are entitled to do so because we are parents, family, teachers, church workers, or adults.

Perhaps the most widely used method of motivation is to play upon the natural desires of power and ambition. These can and do have their place in every person's life. But they should not be used as a manipulative device. Johnny and Anne have enough to cope with without being positively pushed into feeling pride or failure. Aren't we "all members of one body"? Is it right to make Bobby feel superior because he mastered the first-grade reader a year before slower Mary? Is there no way that he can rejoice in the joy of "getting on" for its *own* sake? Is it not materialistic to encourage older children to feel that education is *only* useful for passing exams? Especially when we hammer home that these are the passports to higher salaries? Is this why "higher education" is such a failure that the average US college graduate reads only one book a year?

The Bible *does* give us the picture of a race. The race of life. But the aim is not to beat my brother who runs next to me. It's not that kind of race! I'm not out to show myself better or stronger in any way. Why encourage children to think this way more strongly than they do already? Why lumber some with false pride and handicap others with a false sense of failure? Surely our principle should be to allow the individual to find joy in using his own mind, in learning skills, and in enjoying what others have written (or painted, played, thought; what they did, where they live, etc.).

If you think that the sick fear of not getting an A grade is a lofty means of motivating the child to excellence, I beg to differ. On the contrary, many children fall into a trap of failure, and they try less and less. Others worry more about the grade than about actually learning anything for its own value or for their personal need. They are always focusing on what it looks like to others, rather than on the interest of what they are reading about.

Of course, at some point we all have the uncomfortable test of measuring ourselves against others. Also, it would be wrong to not equip our children with "passports" to our society. There are exams to be passed if Johnny and Ann are to be allowed into the fraternity of our society's demands. But let us try to keep the true spirit of education alive as long as possible. Let us help the child gain skills really well for his own sake, not because of what somebody else can or cannot do. It is *our* responsibility to see that the normal child learns to read, spell, and manipulate numbers with understanding. Often the *child* is blamed for not being teachable at the same rate or by the same means as other children. It is up to the responsible teacher (parent or school) to find ways that *do* work for an individual child.

Can we lead children naturally into excellence in skills and at the same time stimulate their minds with the sheer pleasure of knowledge? If they aren't interested in the material we offer them, something is wrong.

Look at the *material* first. Often school texts are dreary as sawdust. The meat of living books is stripped away, leaving dust-dry bones of fact. A child loves having his mind and imagination captured. School "work" shouldn't be like factory "work" I've heard of, that improves with the use of "games" to stimulate production. For example, after processing thirty bolts in a factory, lights flash, a score lights up, bells ring. It is a profound sadness when the adult's interest and dignity in work is thus exchanged for artificial lollipops. Helpful, alas, because the occupation is so dreary, artificial, repetitious, and long. Doesn't this remind you of many schools?

Secondly, look at the use of *time*. We have become used to the questionable idea that time spent inside four walls "working" equals education. A child is instinctively fidgeting to get at *real* life. Why do we think they are learning more because we are talking at them or because they are writing in workbooks? The child's instinct is wiser than ours.

Teach the skills for their own sake.

Introduce the child to a wide curriculum of living books.

Keep teaching time short enough so that his natural hunger for "real" life can be satisfied.

"Education Is an Atmosphere"

Various types of education can "work." I have personal experience of the educational systems of three countries: the US, Switzerland, and England. One can send a child "through" any system. Each has its own aims, methods, and curricula. We must be tolerant when scrutinizing them, realizing that there is no simple answer to the question of what should be included in "education." We also have to be realistic and remember that by the time Johnny and Anne are eighteen or so they will have to fit into the systems of the country in which they live. The academic English child faces O and A level exams; the American has SAT-type testing for college requirements. The Swiss child has extremely demanding examinations to face if he is to gain entrance to professional training courses or a course of academic study.

Children mature and are successfully educated in other ways. Some, for example, still learn from parents and community as they share in the rural community in Bhutan. These children are startlingly more mature than those graduates from our Western educational institutions. If education can mean different things in different places or times, are there any common denominators? Charlotte Mason suggested three "instruments" of education: the *atmosphere of environment*, the *discipline of habit*, and the *presentation of living ideas*. From my own experience I can vouch for the fact that this combination works.

The Atmosphere of Environment

Charlotte Mason taught that the Christian worldview, properly applied, produces an atmosphere in which the child is accepted just as he is. He does not have to prove himself, pass a test, or show particular talent. He is valuable and unique. He is loved by God, valued and respected by Him.

His mind is not looked down upon; he flourishes in the invigorating atmosphere of sharing truly worthwhile interests with people who like him as a person. His own ideas and choices count. There is an atmosphere of hope and sure expectations. We respect the child's ability to achieve a proper task or skill; there is not the atmosphere of fear or failure. There is an atmosphere of friendship, creativity, and the security produced when human conduct is contained within the boundaries of God's law for us.

This moral atmosphere is not judgmental. The atmosphere is one where parent/child and teacher/pupil are all under the same authority. It is a realistic situation. There is not an atmosphere tense with unreal or perfectionist standards. They can face up to failure and realize that tomorrow will be a new day.

The atmosphere is stimulating because there is a common bond, too, in the area of enjoying knowledge. The atmosphere produced in home or school is a positive one when the adult is eagerly alive to the vital interest in book, subject, activity, or what have you.

I would rather my child had a limited curriculum and access to limited educational resources, and yet learned by basking in the atmosphere of someone who had true pleasure in the books that *were* pursued, than that he should go to some well-equipped and soulless situation where, theoretically, he could "learn" at optimum speed.

The Family

Charlotte Mason believed the family was of prime importance in all child development. The atmosphere in the family comes first.

When we think of the family, we automatically visualize a "stable" family, operating within the plan given by our Creator. A great sadness today is the number of children displaced from the heritage of a united family. It is a God-given plan: a mother, a father, children. On the other hand, an understanding single parent is not barred from having a good family life and home atmosphere. Because they must carefully consider how they will manage, single parents may even provide a richer atmosphere than many preoccupied married couples. There are many different sorts of abnormalities in the fallen world; they set certain limits on what our families can be. Being a single parent is such a handicap, but there are others! Some parents share the homemaking with an alcoholic parent, a workaholic career person, or a superspiritual person who has no time for the "ordinary" things of life. Others have miserable financial, housing, or health problems.

Yet, whatever the abnormalities we face in *our* family, we aim toward an atmosphere of love and forgiveness, within the stability of honoring God's law. In a "good" family, the child gains a deep acceptance, individual value, and a place for creativity while experiencing satisfying relationships. Within a family, the child is not a "job," he is a friend. He contributes in many ways and shares relaxation times.

Charlotte Mason believed that one of the reasons the home is of great educational value is that it isn't an artificial environment. At home, the child can easily make free choices in play and work activities. When the reality of true life hits, you want somebody who is not hothouse bred but is used to the realities and frustrations that are part of home life. For example:

"You have to be quiet, the baby is sleeping."

"Granny is coming, so we won't build a camp in the living room."

"Daddy has had a difficult day, so we aren't going to read a book together now. He's resting. Could you maybe help dry the dishes, so it's nice and tidy when he gets up?"

"Mrs. X is crying because her daughter has cancer. She'll feel comforted if we cook her a good dinner tonight."

"I'm sorry the toddler ruined your model village you built with your blocks. I guess you feel pretty mad! Tomorrow I'll let you build in my bedroom, and we can close the door."

"We miss Daddy. It will never be the same as having a father right here with us. Yet the Lord has promised special help to us in *our* family. He'll help us know what to do."

These real-life situations are educational. Part of reality is that nobody, and no thing, is perfect. Everybody learns from failure too!

The School

Most children in our culture go to school. Here too a similar consideration of the effect of the atmosphere is necessary. When teachers value and trust the individual, a special atmosphere is created. Here it is possible to have structure and yet suitable freedom. The atmosphere can be friendly, purposeful, relaxed. In fact, it can be an oasis for the child who finds it the only place where he is able to have a satisfying life.

The atmosphere is serene and contented when children are not learning out of competition or fear. They are pleased with their own level of skill. They are interested in the good books read to them or by them. They enjoy communicating: speaking (narrating) and writing about what they have read.

The atmosphere is relaxed when children aren't cooped up or organized for too long. There has to be an awareness of the child's need to run, jump, explore, play, and "do," preferably outdoors.

Some people today are ignorant of how well all of this can work. They have perhaps never witnessed the concentration and pleasure of children who are listening to a good book being read aloud. They do not know about the unique atmosphere that exists when children are absorbed in creative activities, including self-motivated play; they do not know about the atmosphere present when there are good, human relationships: where there is respect, trust, order, and time for individuality and work. Some do not even know about the atmosphere of love.

Today we are aware of "good or bad vibes." A child is very sensitive. He knows if he is thought of as a D student, hyperactive, a problem, an intelligent animal, a victim of unhappy circumstances, or as anything rather than a capable, separate person. It is true that atmosphere is produced out of the ideas held by the parents and/or teachers.

By all means, when trying to test the atmosphere of any place where children are to spend time, go and watch. Try to pick up the vibes. But also ask questions: Who is the child? What is your aim in educating him? Do you like children? What are your favorite books, ideas, activities? Do you accept that there are objective standards of right and wrong? Do you think the person is only valuable if he can measure up to some arbitrary norm of achievement? What do you do if your teaching methods fail with an individual child? Do you think he is "bad" if he fails?

And of Christians: Do they enjoy the living reality of a relationship with God and his word? Do they feel impelled to masticate "Christian" matter and give predigested pellets to the children morning, noon, and night? *Do they understand the truth of Christianity?* Do they accept its moral framework, and yet believe in our own independent responsibility? Are they living in a little tiny world, a sort of Christian box? Are they afraid of the breadth of life: its art, music, books, activities—thinking that all life apart from the "spiritual" is "worldly"?

The child should enjoy an atmosphere where life can be explored in a rich way. Little holy hedges are not what is wanted. Understanding the objective certainty of the truth of God gives an atmosphere that is free from fear. We can face up to people's ideas. Questions can be asked. We can talk about them right in the open. Indeed, the child should be able to know, read, or listen to people who hold all sorts of ideas. As they mature, it is absolutely imperative that they be trusted to have access to current "worldly" thought. Some of it has true greatness (say a play, essay, or book). They should be able to enjoy what is good and yet be able to see what ideas are wrong.

This open frank atmosphere can only be achieved when those who produce it are aware of what *is* good, pure, and of a good report (cf. Phil. 4:8).

"Education Is a Discipline"

Let me list a few successes we parents rejoice in when our children manage to produce them (perhaps as listed on a report card!):

> Child X has a habit of attention; he concentrates well. He applies himself to whatever task is at hand, to the best of his ability. He thinks for himself and has a rich creative imagination. He remembers what he has read or heard. He achieves a good standard in his work. He is obedient and careful. He is truthful. He respects others and enjoys his own life with cheerful enthusiasm.

If such a child ever existed, his education would have been unusually successful.

Take *attention* and *concentration*. Why do some children attend while others cannot do so for five minutes in a row?

It is a habit. One child has the habit of attention, and the other never settles easily. He has the habit of restlessness; his mind is like a restless breeze.

Charlotte Mason laid the responsibility not at the child's door but at ours. We have educated him, from babyhood, so that he has helpful habits or unhelpful ones. We can't get away from it.

The habit of a wandering mind may be produced by a chaotic educational setting, where the child is left in a fog of confusion.

It can also be produced when he is "sat down" to weary hours of boring facts or twaddle-type material devoid of interest. Of course his mind wanders!

The habit of a dulled nonthinking mind may be easily produced by sitting the child in front of a TV for long periods.

The habit of noncommunication is also very easily produced. Mix busy adults with little time, and hours spent with large groups of children; add that nobody is especially interested in that particular child's mind or experiences, and you will have, perhaps, a person with no ability to communicate at all.

Or would you like to produce the habit of failure and discouragement? Just put a child into a class where everybody is supposed to learn according to a schedule, not according to individual ability. The child may fall behind because his parents had a bad fight, he missed two weeks of school with an earache, or maybe because he isn't ready to learn that particular step yet. Emotional and physical factors give variables of speed of progress, quite apart from ability or stage of development. So the child misses out. Soon he gets Fs. Are you surprised that he habitually thinks he is dumb or bad or not as good as he should be? Yet another child in this setting will have mastered the offered material some time beforehand. What will *his* interest be? What habits will *he* get into? Jesus said we were not to put a stumbling block in front of "one of these little ones" (Matt. 18:6; Mark 9:42; Luke 17:2). If we burden the child with these mechanical requirements, what other than a stumbling block has our education given him?

There is no escape. It is our duty to consider how we can best help the child to have the right habits. Only then will he be able to easily get on with other people in life, his tasks and responsibilities, his interests, and even his relationship with his Lord.

We have lost sight of the fact that habit is to life what rails are to transport cars. It follows that lines of habit must be laid down towards given ends and after careful survey, or the joltings and delays of life become unsupportable. More, habit is inevitable. If we fail to ease life by laying down of right thinking and right acting, habits of wrong thinking and wrong acting fix themselves of their own accord.[7]

Take the habit of concentration. If this is well-formed, the child is then freed to make a good use of his time. If not, how tiresome every task becomes!

Let's consider a few of these habits as examples.

The Habit of Attention-Concentration

The habit begins with play. The small child *concentrates* on smearing his cereal on the high-chair tray. He later concentrates when you play "This Little Piggy" before his bath. He concentrates on the peekaboo game. He attends to the first book and delights in sitting on your lap and having his favorite books read over and over again. There is time and quiet for him to speak and be listened to; someone who is loved *cares*.

The story-reading time is extended as he matures. He has a habit of listening for longer and longer periods of time. Suitable books engross his interest, and he is used to talking about what he has heard. Meanwhile, he is given skills to learn. When he is ready, he'll be thrilled to learn to read for himself. There is peace and order for this important step. He learns the sounds the letters make; he has plenty of practice in sounding out words. He enjoys practicing writing. The time spent on this is short enough to prevent the habit of mind-wandering from setting in.

Children differ, of course. Some will gain the habit of concentration and attention more easily than others. It behooves us to understand how this can be encouraged, so as to help those who find it more difficult.

The Habit of Truthfulness

Make it easy for the child to tell the truth in small ways. Help him to learn to be exact and particular about the truth. Sometimes a habit of untruthfulness begins because of a general attitude that it doesn't matter or that it is acceptable to be foggy. Help a child focus on what has happened, help him to report it exactly. This will help him to get into the habit of being truthful.

"Alice, please could you check on how many bottles of milk are left and come and tell me?" Alice is pleased to be asked and skips off with four-year-old eagerness to see.

"Bob, please tell Dad that the garden seeds cost $12.50. See if he can give us the extra $2.50, as I only have $10.00." Bob is learning that detail matters, he is pleased at being trusted, and he importantly departs on his task.

We shouldn't wait for the really hard test of "owning up" to some wrongdoing to try to teach the habit of truth. We have to be honest and open ourselves. We have to practice trust in the family and school, in lots of little ways, all the time. This is the basis of human relationships. Our example is our heavenly Father, whom we may trust at all times. He never lets us down. He has openly shared the truth with us. It matters.

The Habit of Self-Control

When an adult is depressed, it often helps him to start some program of exercise: jogging, swimming, or what have you. The fitness makes you feel better, but you also gain an encouraging sense of self-control. This helps you "ride the storm," however the tides are flowing. This idea of self-conquest is central. The child needs to learn, both as an idea and also in practice, that we are not buffeted merely by our feelings.

"But I don't *want* to!" is a cry, not only when I am six, but just as much when I am sixty.

We need to quietly and cheerfully push the selfish "I want" out of the center of our lives. This is also a habitual reaction. The question should be not, "What do I want," but "What do I think is *right* in this instance?" This habit helps children cope with their wills.

As parents and then teachers, we have golden opportunities for helping a child have the habit of not pushing himself constantly into the center.

To help the will be a strong instrument in helping us do what is right, the demands must be realistic. It is cruel to ask a young child to share a new and precious toy when he is longing to hold and protect the cherished possession. Make the tasks easy and only gradually harder. Life itself is the best teacher in this. We have no need to invent extra burdens! "I know that you'd like to go out and play, but it's cold and your ear infection isn't over yet. Look, here is a new lump of play dough." This adult is expressing the reality of a situation. But he is making it easier for the child to will his attention away from what he wants to what is an alternative. A diversion has been offered.

"I can see you don't feel like working on your arithmetic. But it is your duty to try as hard as you can. When twenty minutes are up, you can stop. If you finish the page sooner, you will be able to go and play with the LEGOs."

"I can see that you want to hurt John. You can't hit him with that stick. That is wrong, however you feel. You can shout and make a noise to let him see how angry you are. But I think you've already done that! You are going to have your bath now, so come away with me, and you can tell me what he did that makes you feel like this."

The Habit of Unselfishness

Perhaps this is a central area for we who live in the late twentieth century. The demand "I want" rules supreme. The atmosphere of not having one's self at the center is necessary, and adults should be aware of this for themselves first. It's sometimes good to express just how you feel, so that children realize that you too have different desires from your daily duties! It's good to say cheerfully, "Boy, I wish that I didn't have to work this morning! After all that rain, the sun makes me want to drop everything and go out to the beach. But I know that I have to work inside this morning."

It is also good to verbalize the little victories the child gains over his "I wants." For instance, "Joel, you made little Peter really happy when you let him play with your train" or "Jane, I could see that you wanted to quit your work. I think you did a really good job finishing it all before you ran out to play."

It *is* possible to help the child, to help him to be the sort of mature adult who knows that he can choose to do what he doesn't always feel like doing.

To develop this habit, it shouldn't be too obvious a burden. Understand the child's needs. Meet them. Let them "be their age." But in many small ways, this way of thinking and acting should be encouraged, practiced, and become a part of life.

In the school of life, we are all pupils in these matters. We should consider how we can apply habit-formation both at home and at school. Bad habits make slaves of those who have them. But good habits are like tracks along which our usual behavior runs. This frees us to concentrate on the important choices we have to make in life.

Routines form habits. They are frameworks we can think about. We can make priorities. Yes, going to church or reading the Bible and praying can be decried as being just empty habits. But how helpful the habit is! Then, it is the *reality* of what we make of what we usually do that counts.

Take the area of human relationships. Routines do not *make* the relationship. But they are the frame upon which we can hang our experiences. Some families do not have a routine of eating meals together anymore. Anytime goes for snacking; people rush about at a thousand activities, any one of which could be good. But what is the sum total? Without the priority of a framework, nothing much happens: few conversations, little time of togetherness. A family decides to read a book together "whenever there is time." This invariably becomes no time. It is essential to have these basic routines. Having them does not devalue experience. The same is true when we encourage habits of politeness and respect to each other. For instance, words like *please* and *thank you* are important. Mutual consideration is an essential part of life.

Structure and Form

On this model, the child starting a school day gets out his books knowing that while his mind is fresh, there will be quietness to concentrate on the central skills of reading, writing, and numbers. Children love routines. It frees their attention for the activity at hand. Later on, other routines help the child along. One part of each day, according to Charlotte Mason, will be lots of time "to himself." Part of the routine is free time. He looks forward to the family meal at home, knowing that he will be able to talk about everything that is happening to him. At the end of the day, there may be the routine of listening to a book being read aloud, reading the Bible, praying.

When planning routines, priority must be given to the most important things. The person matters (be it child, husband/wife, or friend). We'll need *time* to talk, read, relax, and work together. Our relationship with God matters. Where is the time to be found for that? I am a part of this creation. Where will I find time to get out and enjoy nature? There is too much work to be done, and I am finite. I need to accept that reality and plan the time and priorities carefully.

The child is not isolated within some sort of developmental program. We all share in life together. We learn from each other. And when we make correct decisions, the child in our care benefits from being helped to good habits, good priorities, and good routines.

Who can hope to "arrive" or be successful? None of us is able to say, "Yes, I have." It helps us to accept our own weakness, our own needs, our own limitations. We have to operate within the limits of what is possible. It will never be perfect. But it is wonderful not to be merely swept along by feelings and circumstances.

One should also feel free to alter a given routine. How refreshing to announce, "Tonight it's so lovely we're going to skip supper and chores! Let's go to the woods to play and stop for some hamburgers and milkshakes to take with us."

Or in school, "Let's not do our work this morning. Why don't we take the day off to build a dam in the stream?"

When Charlotte Mason had her training college for teachers, on some exceptionally fine mornings a bell would ring. The young students' eyes would sparkle. They would set off on an all-day expedition to some valley or lake in the beautiful English Lake District.

It often rains there, and if you planned ahead for a special day off, it would no doubt be raining. Life is short, and sunny moments need to be snatched. Sometimes it is the children's idea. "Please," a pair of entreating eyes may plead, "couldn't we go camping this weekend?" or go to the woods, or read an extra chapter, or stay up late so as to see Granny arrive?

Duty calls, and responsibility should be accepted habitually. But it should be balanced with the liberty to enjoy life. Did not our Lord enjoy the wheat kernels in the fields on the Sabbath? (See Luke 6:1–5.)

Surely we can say: the child is not made for education, but education is to serve the child, serve his personality, his life, his needs.

"Education Is a Life"

Education is a life. That life is sustained on ideas. Ideas are of spiritual origin, and God has made us so that we get them chiefly as we convey them to one another, whether by word of mouth, written page, Scripture word, musical symphony; but we must sustain a child's inner life with ideas as we sustain his body with food.[8]

Consider for a moment what we plan to offer to the child. We know that when we feed his physical body, it is important that we do not give him only calories. For proper growth, the body needs a balanced diet, providing protein, vitamins, fiber, etc.

And yet, this child is often spiritually and mentally starved. This is another reason why certain children are driven to strange and unnatural behavior. They have been deprived of the life which is their heritage.

Our Lord spoke of abundant life (John 10:10). He said, "Man does not live on bread alone" (Matt. 4:4). Nor does he live by being reared on a computer printout, or scientifically planned workbooks that build skills by reading comprehension exercises based on isolated paragraphs, or any of the horrors that sometimes go under the name of "the education process."

What a violence it would be to the child, to conscientiously apply the "habit" and "discipline" ideas of education and then to sit them down routinely to meals of sawdust!

"Let the children at the best of life!" is Charlotte Mason's challenge to us. Life includes not only living experiences but also the best that mankind has produced in art, books, music, ideas, and many more areas.

When I was seven years old, I arrived in a war-torn Europe, straight from the rather sterile niceness of middleclass mid-America. I was a very average, ordinary little tomboy girl! One afternoon I was taken into the Rijksmuseum, and I walked right up to Rembrandt's painting, *Night Watch*. Did the guards smile as a little girl tarried there for a long, long time? Nobody lectured me as to what I was supposed to know or think about this painting. I was not disturbed. I was left alone with Rembrandt. A magical contact! I still remember the paintings I saw in Holland as if I had been there last week instead of thirty-five years ago, when I commented, "If somebody would give me enough paint, I would paint a picture like that!" Adults may have smiled. But I had found a human link with a kindred spirit.

Let children feed on the good, the excellent, the great! Don't get in their way with little lectures, facts, and guided tours! Lift a preschool child onto your lap, and look together at a full-page color reproduction of some great painting, drawing, or etching. Enjoy it, talk and notice together the details the child points to. Let the *child* look, enjoy with you; let *him* respond.

Children respond to the very best music. Get recordings of Brahms, Bach, Beethoven, Elgar, and Mendelssohn. Play them to a three-year-old; maybe the child will dance, clap, smile. Let children beat drums or march.

There is no need to start them off on a watery diet of musically-poor fare. Give them the best! Let a few works become friends. Then get good seats at a concert. Sit up close. See the child stare in wonder as the violinist plays, the conductor conducts, and the choir sings. If you have taken care that at least one item in the program is familiar to the child already, you will probably feel an excited tug and hear, "Listen, they are playing *our* music!"

A L'Abri student, who read this book in manuscript, returned to her Texas public school determined to use some of Charlotte Mason's ideas with her second- and third-grade classes. She began to play a few carefully chosen recordings regularly at rest time. Soon the children were eagerly asking for "the Vivaldi," "the Beethoven," "the Brahms." They weren't aware that they were learning. Something new, a richness, had been given to them, and they enjoyed it.

Share good books with the children. It is a magic door of contact between the child and some of the most interesting and creative people our culture has enjoyed. Let them know the authors by reading to them their living books. Textbooks hardly ever fall into this category. Charlotte Mason never looked down on a child's reaction to such books. She simply devoted a great deal of effort to ensuring that the child had access to living books. Such books stimulate ideas—that electrifying confrontation that touches the center of the person. Ideas stimulate discussion, interest, and involvement.

Do not forget that the reading of the Bible will put the child into direct contact with the person of God himself. The brief, pithy statement or narration of Scripture is often worth ten sermons! Let the words themselves sink in. Don't chew up the ideas yourself and then hand over the half-digested "food" to the child. Let him have direct access to the source.

We don't have to chart exactly what a child has "learned" from any of these sources to make it worthwhile using them. This is a different way of thinking about learning. Our job is to give the best nourishment regularly. The child takes what is appropriate to him at that time. A good example is when we enjoy a book together as a family. The nine-year-old enjoys hearing J. R. R. Tolkien's *The Lord of the Rings*. He extracts nourishment for mind and spirit. The fourteen-year-old also is fed but extracts something different. The parents enjoy it in yet another way. There is no "right" way to react, no list of items one has to remember. Living life isn't like that. We are individuals, and we leave it that way.

Although we should give a child access to varied creative work by other people, how about seeing that he grows up with as much daily access as possible to his Lord's created works? The Bible is a direct verbal word. But we have a place also for other ways of knowing him, for "the heavens declare the glory of God" (Ps. 19:1).

Do the children know the feel of dew-fresh grass on their bare feet and lush freshness of the shade of a leafy tree on a hot afternoon? Do they know the fun of autumn leaves and the fairy-tale beauty of an icy morning? Wherever the child lives in the world, we should consider his contact with nature as part of his life.

How do we shortchange the child of today? We coop him up like a battery hen in a gaudy plastic cage. We "timetable" his day with "improving" activities so that he is a foreigner to himself and to the great outdoors.

We should open the door to understanding the wonder of the physical world. Science is often so highly specialized that we shy off. We should realize that the wholeness of reality is a unity which is an exciting part of life. And so we should try to see that a child can wonder at the incredibly interesting structure of God's world. Direct contact is possible and interesting: watch crystals grow, or wonder over the snowflake seen through a magnifying glass. There is wonder all around us if we'll look, touch, and try.

But there is much that we cannot see. Children naturally want to *know*.

"What makes the light come on?"

"How does the daddy's seed get into the mother?"

"Why don't satellites fall down?"

"Where does the snow go in summer?"

There are beautiful books which tell about the interesting world around us. If you (the adult) read the text, you can hold the small child on your lap and look at the pictures. You can then share what you have learned from your reading. (Not a whole lecture, just an interesting explanation of what is illustrated—short and to the point.)

An older child will sit fascinated as you read the text or parts of it. Lots of discussion will follow—it keeps you on your toes!

Charlotte Mason's ideal world for children had nature at the doorstep. She felt that organized lessons should only take up the morning, so that children could freely play in and enjoy the gardens, meadows, woods, and lanes of England every afternoon.

What of children in cities, where adults fear violence, and the child is not safe playing alone, especially in the parks? What of the child in the city school, where there is no nature to be seen?

Another L'Abri student who has read this book has gone back to an inner city to help plan camps where children will acquire some memories of the countryside, and this is good.

A church may decide that instead of more meetings, it will bus its children into nearby countryside once a month. It is a priority that children should be allowed to enjoy God's environment. They should be taken to a safe place where they can choose to build camps, learn to swim, follow maps, paint, etc. At least one day in the month would be theirs in which to explore, jump, imagine, wonder, smell Spring coming.

A school reschedules lessons to leave the afternoon free. One group takes over a weedy patch of ground and carefully succeeds in making a city farm. Vegetables are grown, chickens lay eggs, a goat is milked. Other children reclaim a neglected park under their teacher's supervision. They help to make it beautiful and then get to play under the trees. The adults may think it a poor exchange for a "perfect setting," but the child's imagination ignores the traffic fumes. It's grass to play on anyway, and the leaves fall in satisfyingly crunchy piles in the fall. Ants crawl along the path. Birds flock to a feeding table in winter.

The less a child is surrounded by nature, the more creative the adults must be to allow the child *some* contact with it.

Education is a *life*.

Part of the child's life consists of mixing with different kinds of people or experiencing different situations. Have you ever taken the children to spend some time with a seriously handicapped person? If you live on the leafy outskirts of a city, do your children have any opportunities to build friendships with people who live in the inner city? Or with old people? If you are Christians, do they *know* anybody who has very different beliefs? If you are white, how many black people do your children know? If you are black, how many white people? Not just know superficially, either, but know as *persons*. Abraham Lincoln spent only one year in school. The rest of his youth, he read books, he worked, and on the Mississippi River, he met all sorts of people. He knew them. In fact, his life *educated* him.

Sadly, many schools and families today are not sources of life in this area. We often fail to put children in touch with a wide cross section of people. We like neat compartments. Five-year-olds here, people with intellectual disabilities there, oversixties in the afternoons.

Children in cities may have trouble having satisfying contact with nature, but do we make the use we could of *people*? They are interesting, and there are a lot of them! For example, the Vietnamese who runs a small business may let the youngster help out. They might talk. They might both really learn something.

One of the advantages my children had when they left school and were educated at home was that they had time to mix with a wider cross-section of people than before. They weren't shut away with thirty other ten-year-olds all day.

One day Ranald John would come back with war stories he had heard from an old man he had met in the village. It was better than a documentary. This was *real*!

Another day Fiona told how an old lady delivered milk fifty years ago in a donkey cart. Both children had time to make friendships with all sorts of people—time to talk and help too. Time to play with younger children and care for babies.

Of course, many realize the educational power of putting children in contact with other people. But the child has to have real contact, a real relationship. Successful programs have, for instance, set adolescents to painting and gardening for old folk.

Others have helped children with intellectual disabilities to read and taught blind children to swim.

Churches could be centers where people get to know each other, discuss, learn, and give in a way that cuts through artificial divisions like race, sex, health, intelligence, and age.

Life includes *other people.*

Work

Part of life is the aspect of work and responsibility. When a child is at home, he wants to share in the activities that are obviously important: the work going on. The two-year-old says, "Me too! Me wash the floor. Me stir the ice cream." Children are drawn in as interested spectators when machines are mended, food is cooked, ditches are dug, and so on. Then they enjoy joining in!

One sad aspect of our century is the complexity that prevents a child from sharing work. So we contrive artificial situations, such as measuring and weighing, to make up for it.

Whenever possible, a child should partake in real work situations. Children like company and variety in work, and there should never be so much to do that the all-important play/free growing time is excluded. However, if the school hours are shorter and more valuable, there is time for work and play. Inner-city Free Schools in London have given a living interest to bored twelve-year-old boys by letting one or two at a time work on cars in a garage. These same boys also enjoy preparing food for the group. They'll chip in and take responsibility.

In trying to give a child a carefree existence, we often leave him stranded with meaningless tasks. A sensitive balance must be established so that the routine of a child's life is not burdened with work responsibilities that rob him of a childhood growing time. Yet, they love to participate in the work just as others do.

Creativity

A student at L'Abri once asked, "How do you get children to be creative?" In fact, we can't *teach* creativity. Children respond to life, each in his own individual way. How interesting to stand back and watch! Provide a *time* and *place*. It helps if they are allowed access to paper, wood, costumes, and so on. Children used to improvise creatively much more effectively without the fancy clutter which often takes away imagination today. Steer clear of coloring books. Provide good art paper, paint, markers, pencils, pens. Encourage creativity by your appreciation of what is produced.

Let children make music. Listen to their stories and poetry. If a child isn't ready to write down his own thoughts yet, let him dictate them to you. The habit of putting thoughts into words will come in handy later when your creative writer actually writes well enough to do it himself!

Allow children to work in kitchens. Let them be creative with food and cooking. Even chopping vegetables is satisfying.

Let them handle clay, wood, and lovely materials. Let them learn to sew and be adept in all sorts of crafts.

Free time is necessary for the fruit of creativity. It grows out of the rich life that has been the subject of this chapter. All children respond to this abundance with ideas, plans, imagination, playing. They solve problems, think, grow. Children respond to life by living. They need this time to grow.

Education is an *atmosphere*, a *discipline*, a *life*.

5

Education: A Science
of Relationships

WHEN I WAS A CHILD, education for me often meant memorizing French verbs or remembering someone else's answer to a question. Now I find it helpful and liberating to enjoy Charlotte Mason's view of education. It does not mean that adults think of a child as a blank sheet of paper on which they imprint their ideas, impressions, and knowledge. Neither does it mean leaving the child unattended like a weed growing in a sidewalk. It is a balanced understanding of education as the provision of possibilities for a person to build relationships with a vast number of things and thoughts.

We must take steps to provide a diet which opens doors for each child to build a relationship with God, other persons, and the universe. If it sounds broad, it *is* broad! A child should not be left to stumble upon educational material by chance. Charlotte Mason took great care to provide a wide variety of curriculum. Otherwise the child will be deprived of the best in ideas, culture, literature, science, etc.

Whether the relationships which make up education are fostered in or out of school doesn't matter. One child has "the door of books" opened by an imaginative sixth-grade teacher who loves literature. Another child would have never learned to love reading if it hadn't been for a neighbor who read him *Hurry Home Candy* one winter's night. This child will be introduced to the existence of a Creator God who loves the child individually by his uncle who takes him fishing. That child is put in touch with an aspect of truth at home by his parents, and yet another child learns this at school from a teacher.

The precise mix of the places where the child is put in touch with different areas of reality will differ from child to child, even within one family. Therefore, we need to extend the concept of the "rich curriculum" as being given *outside* as well as *in* school. It is the balance of the entire offering which counts, not the place where each bit happens. Education is taking place during all of the waking hours.

Knowledge of God: Putting a Child in Touch with the God Who Is There

Of the three sorts of knowledge proper to a child, the knowledge of God, of man, and of the universe,—the knowledge of God ranks first in importance, is indispensable and most happy-making.[1]

Our first concern is to open the door to the knowledge of God. The small child first becomes aware of the loving and just Father through his own parents' love and ordered care for him. In his joy of discovery, his eager mind blossoms. A parent who knows that God is not an emotional projection or a psychological hope will almost unconsciously include the existence of God in the worldview and the atmosphere of life with which he surrounds the child.

Just as the small child quickly learns by being in the company of parents who enjoy music, for example, so will he pick up the reality of a relationship when he sees his mother simply praying or his dad quietly worshiping in church week by week. This reality is central to "the bundle of life" we share with our children.

Children listen to the conversations taking place around them. They soon notice that when issues are talked about they relate to the Christian framework in some way, quite naturally. They learn that direct questions like "Who made the stars?" have a simple and perfectly truthful answer: "God." By many such matter-of-fact, relaxed conversations, they sense with certainty that their parents are secure in the framework God has given.

I think little children are put off by too much intense talk. This happens when an earnest father gives his four-year-old son a ten-minute lecture on steam trains when all the boy wanted was the simple answer, "Coal is burned. It heats the water, that makes steam, and that is how the steam train goes." When a distressed child asks the question, "Where did the cat go when he died?" and gets an intense sermon by way of an answer, the child soon stops asking!

If a child is respected, one does not talk down to him. One can give simple and quick answers that are genuine. Honesty is another rule. "I'm not sure" or "I don't know" are helpful replies when such is the case.

This leads to a most important principle. We ourselves are fellow sheep. We shouldn't act as if we ourselves are the source material for the child. We are to put the child into direct contact with the one Lord who communicated with us.

The expressed knowledge attainable by us has its source in the Bible, and perhaps we cannot do a greater indignity to children than to substitute our own or some other benevolent person's rendering for the fine English, poetic diction, and lucid statement of the Bible.[2]

So we need not necessarily produce "religious" material for the curriculum. It is simple and right to include the reading of Scripture in the daily plan, both at home and/or at school.

The PNEU schools followed a consecutive plan of Bible reading. The Gospels, the epistles, Revelation, and the Old Testament were included. The passages were carefully chosen. The child was put in touch with the men and women who found God worked into the history of their lives.

The reading was simply prepared. If there was a new name or place, this would first be explained briefly. One could look on a map to see the location and perhaps have a short descriptive account of the place or custom. The previous reading would be briefly recalled.

Then the passage was read. It wouldn't be too long, but it would be long enough to draw the listener into the story, ideas, or poetry. At the close, someone in the class would narrate what he had heard.

The word of God is like fertile seed you drop into the soil. The child does not take in everything that is there. He thinks about some aspect of it. "An idea strikes him" or he "feels" (knowledge touched with emotion). He thinks. He "chews on some part of it."

And that is that.

Charlotte Mason warns us against exhausting the child with endless nagging exhortations to "be good." She reminds us that first must come a personal knowledge of the truth, which is what makes us strive for good.

> Let us save Christianity for our children by bringing them into allegiance to Christ, the King. How? How did the old Cavaliers bring up sons and daughters, in passionate loyalty and reverence for not too worthy princes? Their own hearts were full of it; their lips spake it; their acts proclaimed it; the style of their clothes, the ring of their voices, the carriage of their heads—all was one proclamation of boundless devotion to their king and his cause . . . what shall we say of "the Chief amongst ten thousand, the altogether lovely"?[3]

The reality of the *life* lived keeps coming in, as well as giving the child direct access to the word.

She then goes on to advise us to remember to also bring the child to "Jesus, our Saviour."

We all sin. It is discouraging. It also is a guilt trap. Very early on, a child himself cries out with Paul, "What I want to do I do not do, but what I hate I do" (Rom. 7:15). The child needs to know that his burden too can "roll off his back." Jesus has paid the penalty for the guilt of all who say, "Yes, thank you," to him.

A child is glad to know he is safely accepted because of the work of the Savior. He loves knowing that he belongs.

We should make it possible for the child to know the "King-Savior-Child" relationship in simple confidence. We are always to "let the little children come to me, and do not hinder them, for the kingdom of heaven belongs to such as these" (Matt. 19:14). If we do not tell them, how shall they come? And do we not also forbid them, when we cover up the vital reality of our Lord and

King, by turning this joyful simple access into a dull, weary, and unending verbal sermon?

The child should also hear and know of the Father, to whom he is led in Jesus's name in his simple daily prayer. He should hear of the Holy Spirit, who is given to help us in every part of our life.

All of this is so important that we walk a delicate line. We ourselves need to pray to the Lord for wisdom. We should not overdo our own enthusiasm, or the children will hear too much talk on the matter, and they will be tired of it. The Bible reading should be definite, clear, and yet not wearisome. Likewise, prayer should be sincere and conversation genuine. Another input is to introduce children to other Christians through the reading of interesting biographies and books. When I was young, I benefited by having as my "friends" Isobel Kuhn and Amy Carmichael. I met them as my mother and father read their books to us on Sunday evenings. But do not make the mistake of thinking that to counteract this present secular society one should fill every day with more and yet more "Christian" material. You will surely hinder the child this way!

A child should have his own beautiful and well-printed Bible. He will delight in reading you a portion. In the PNEU program, the children were also given Psalms of appropriate lengths to memorize. Again, in its place, this is enjoyed by children. And what a treasure it gives them! I still recall passages learned as a child in moments of adult stress.

We deal with positive truth. But there are also negative threats. Societies and ideas are being turned upside-down:

> Nor is a social revolution the only one pending. There is a horror of great darkness abroad, Christianity is on its trial; and more than that, the most elementary belief in, and worship

of, Almighty God. The judgment to come, the resurrection of the body, the life everlasting—these fundamental articles of a Christian's faith have come to be poohpoohed; and this, not only among profane persons and ungodly livers, but amongst people of reputation both for goodness and wisdom.

And how are the young [girls] to be prepared to meet this religious crisis? In the first place, it is unwise to keep them in the dark as to the anxious questions stirring.[4]

And so, Charlotte Mason is not so far away from us. We are just further down the road. We are surrounded by a post-Christian culture. We do not have to submerge our children in the morass of murky non-Christian society to let them know what the "anxious questions" are. Is there rock music on the radio? They should not be allowed to merely be surrounded by a voiceless noisy din. Somebody should sit down with the youngsters and listen to the words. In that way the *ideas* can be discussed together. Let them *think*. Their reading should include literature which expresses the dilemma of the non-Christian. They will have questions and want to talk about the basic ideas.

It must, however, be kept in mind that certain products of our culture are so corrupt that children must be protected. Video, movies, or TV are at times merely hell on a screen. Surely there can never be any excuse for exposing young people to the sight of such evil. There is a balance. When I say that children and young people need to hear something of the world around them, I do not mean that they should be allowed to drag through the mire of everything in our culture.

Some things can be enjoyed as a Christian. Others must be discussed and understood. A third category must be avoided.

People often say to me, "What really impresses me about the L'Abri story wasn't the people who came, but that you children 'carried on' without rebelling. I'd like to know what your parents did?"

Well, lots of Christian parents also have their prayers for their children answered in the same way. They have also adapted creatively to their situations. There is never a magic formula. Each child makes choices, both good and bad. The Holy Spirit works with each one of us.

But there are some aspects of my childhood that I can point to. We had a sound grounding in God's word. We shared in life with our parents, and they became people who dared to trust God. We saw prayers answered. It wasn't theory. We could talk about real questions and discuss possible answers together. If there were problems, we weren't kept in the dark. We knew about the ideas behind the "anxious questions" while our childhood gave us the sort of wholesome life Charlotte Mason talks about. That helped protect us from being dragged down by peer pressure. But we not only heard about other ideas, we met all sorts of people. We could sit up and hear the conversation of a brilliant atheist, a teenage agnostic, and a Hindu. We could see the despair of the existentialist and ache with the lostness of someone who was trying to live as if he wasn't made as a human being. We could listen to the logic of the Christian ideas as they were discussed. We could see where the ideas of the other point of view led: "If what you say is true, then . . ." Often the conclusions of the humanist argument simply didn't fit reality or just couldn't work.

We weren't forced to listen in. No! Often it would be regarded as a special treat to "stay up and hear . . . just one more hour, *please.*"

I think that any community has people whose ideas will prove just as interesting when we invite them home and talk. It is the ideas and the people who matter not being in a special place.

Such honest questioning demands good answers. That is why we have to use the minds we've been given.

But let their zeal be according to knowledge. Lay the foundation of their faith. [Details of individual opinion matter less than] that they should know fully in Whom they have believed, and what are the grounds of their belief. Put earnest, *intellectual* works into their hands. Let them feel the necessity of bracing up every power of mind they have to gain comprehension of the breadth and the depth of the truths they are called to believe. Let them not grow up with the notion that Christian literature consists of emotional appeals, but that intellect, mind, is *on the other side.* Supply them with books of calibre to give the intellect something to grapple with—an important consideration, for the danger is, that young people in whom the spiritual life is not yet awakened should feel themselves superior to the vaunted simplicity of Christianity.[5]

Here is a word of wisdom. Charlotte Mason addresses those who have been educating children on nutritious mind-food. These young people are used to reading nonfrivolous matter so that they can "grapple intellectually." This isn't talking about stuff that is "intellectual for intellectualism's sake" but deep consideration of questions, ideas, and answers.

The young person should not be left to base his Christian faith on the inadequate foundation of "emotional appeals." On the contrary: our minds can look full into the face of the basic questions, and the implications of Christianity can—and do—stand firmly as reasonable. I have the personal joy of seeing this worked out in young persons' lives for the last twenty-two years that I have worked in L'Abri.

Mind is on our side. It is liberating, wonderful, and produces healthy growth. We don't have to keep our Christianity in a little compartment labeled "faith." It fits reality. There are good answers, good reasons. The light of truth shines brightly.

Perhaps it is in this way that the Christian church has injured its young people most deeply. It has often not given, on the one hand, the sure and definite foundation of objective biblical teaching. Then it has tended to close its mind to the intellectual cry of the mind: "Where is God?" "Why do we see evil if he is good?" "Does modern science disprove Christianity?" "Are the biblical documents reliable?"

On top of this, we have tolerated a separation between the "secular" and the "religious." Thus people have had to close their minds to all other aspects of life and intellectual questions when they entered the "faith" box or that of "experience." It is as if they were called upon to leave philosophy, literary questions, art, social questions, historical views, political action, science, and so on in a sort of mental parking lot outside the "religious experiences." Charlotte Mason allowed no such division between the "secular" and the "religious." She understood that the *whole* of reality is part of God's reality.

She often referred to a medieval painting (a fresco in the church of Santa Maria Novella) which struck her on a visit to Florence. In it she saw depicted the Holy Spirit inspiring the various "departments" of human endeavor. Art, mathematics, and so on—all are part of the whole life, reality. We can and should appreciate, execute, and learn about art, music, literature, history, math, science, philosophy, and so on—*for their own sakes.*

Often climbers are asked, "Why do you climb Mount Everest?" The answer comes quickly. "Because it is there."

In the same way, the inquiry "Why do you study, or do math, art, etc.?" should be swiftly answered by "Because it is part of the whole, which God has created."

Charlotte Mason and my dad, Francis A. Schaeffer, would have agreed deeply on this point:

> True spirituality covers all of reality. There are things the Bible tells us as absolutes which are sinful—which do not conform to the character of God. But aside from these the Lordship of Christ covers *all* of life and *all* of life equally. In this sense there is nothing concerning reality that is not spiritual.
>
> Related to this, it seems to me, is the fact that many Christians do not mean what I mean when I say Christianity is true, or Truth. They are Christians and they believe in, let us say, the truth of creation, the truth of the virgin birth, the truth of Christ's miracles, Christ's substitutionary death, and His coming again. But they stop there with these and other individual truths.
>
> When I say Christianity is true I mean it is true to total reality—the total of what is, beginning with the central reality, the objective existence of the personal-infinite God. Christianity is not just a series of truths but *Truth*—Truth about all of reality. And the holding of that Truth intellectually—and then in some poor way living upon the truth, the Truth of what is—brings forth not only certain personal results, but also governmental and legal results.[6]

One clear result is that of an educational philosophy.

I have put this consideration in this chapter on the "Christian" aspect of education for a reason. Some believe that to secure a "Christian" education, one has to use Christian textbooks for study.

It is a mistake to think that arithmetic problems are more "Christian" if, for example, the child sticks to measurements of the ark! No, measurement is part of reality, to be studied *for its own sake*. The child should be put in touch with the best available material in each field. So, the math program we choose will probably have been written by someone with a quite different religious view from the Christian one. Math does relate to the whole of truth; it has its place. It is like art, music, horticulture, or cooking: the "Christian-ness" of it lies in itself. We are secure in God's truth, which is a framework into which we can fit all the parts of reality.

When teaching the Calvert School home instruction course to my ten-year-old, we both benefited enormously from Hillyer's *A Child's History of the World*. Hillyer knows more about the pageant of history than I ever will. His book is enjoyable while being informative. In reading his book we learned about the broad flow of history, its peoples, ideas, events. At last I read why Hannibal crossed the Alps! A grasp of such facts plus an interest in ideas stimulated lively thinking and discussion. Then I used the film series *How Should We Then Live?* to give a Christian's view of, say, the French Revolution or the Romans.

There are many ways of applying the "Christianity that is true to the total reality." We don't have to make every day a sort of Sunday school lesson to achieve this. There are several dangers in that sort of approach. Too much pious talk, talk, talk. Too many "holy moments." Expecting continual religious experiences. Not letting children "be." Not letting them wonder, puzzle, and ask.

On the other side, we live in a time when our culture is all-invading, all-persuasive. The population, as a whole, is led like a pig with a ring in its snout. Unthinking opinions are the order of the day. The consensus of opinion is more important than what is right or true. Secular humanists preach that there is such a thing as a neutral stance, yet *their* worldview comes over loud and clear as the "obvious" one. We live in a passive age. "Let the experts decide" about the ethics of abortion, the practices of the educational system, the legality of family laws.

It is an imperative priority, as never before, to allow our children to learn to think, understand, and see the central truths quite explicitly and clearly. *This* is a central part of the "Christian" aspect of our education.

We were able to show the film series *Whatever Happened to the Human Race?* to our daughter's school. Attendance was optional. The children were between thirteen and sixteen years old, from average homes. They were absolutely riveted by the ideas of who the person is and his worth, and the topics of euthanasia, abortion, old age, and so on. Discussion afterward was lively and penetrating. Children need to consider practical issues. They want to think. They want *answers*. Christianity is part of that rock of reality about which youngsters long to know. They need to understand how contemporary issues fit into what the Bible says.

Have you read *The Plague* by Camus with a group of fifteen-year-olds? Have they wondered over the problem of evil, the human problem? In reading this novel, do they notice the fallacy of the priest's argument? "God has willed this child to suffer." Do they think about how different the biblical perspective is: that the suffering was unleashed by man's choice to disobey God? That all individuals and the course of history are caught up in this river of consequence—an abnormal world?

Do they read *Brave New World* and discuss the logical conclusion of the humanist view of man, his morality, humanity, and social purpose?

Can they pick up something like *Time* magazine, read it, and think about where it fits into the Christian framework?

Do they come home from school, or from having seen a TV program, and spontaneously discuss what is right, what is wrong?

Have they thrashed through the reasons why the Bible is true? Do they understand the fallacies of other positions? Can they remember numerous occasions when the Bible was seen to fit like a key into the keyhole of reality? Do they know about the historical and archaeological evidence? Are they amazed at how the philosophical ideas of the Bible fit into the way we find reality to be?

They should not be left with only a feeling—"I know it's true because I feel it in my heart." That is not enough.

One morning they will wake up, and you will be gone and so will their feelings.

Do they *know*?

All of this is "Christian education."

Seeing fallacies. Understanding. Knowing the Bible. Thinking. Judging ideas. Seeking and keeping ears open. Being in touch.

Perhaps it is well to end on the why of teaching Christian truth. We do not become Christians because it will make us happy. Nor because we believe it will be a passport to a sugarcoated life.

We are called to one who *is there*. We respond because that *is right* and appropriate.

When set firmly on the ground of reality, we will indeed experience our own relationship with a personal God who is there. It will alter the quality and experience of my life. I will be called to serve. I am commanded to place the Lord King at the center of my life. In serving him, I am then to serve others. It is this perspective that is passed onto the next generation.

Having given the basis for the knowledge, plus a place for the telling of ideas or discussion, please allow each child to live his own private life. We tend to crash in where angels fear to tread. We want to push along the work that belongs to the Holy Spirit.

Let the child do his own living—*please*!

I once witnessed a pathetic scene. A determined father was "teaching" his toddler to "enjoy" the sea. The babe was firmly carried into the breakers and plonked into a cold foaming, crashing world. Poor wee mite! She protested loudly with cries. The father had a "you have to enjoy this or else" look on his face. The child was forced to "play" in the water. The terror, unpleasantness, and force probably left that child with a lifelong dislike of water, the ocean in particular. When you take a toddler to the beach, you don't follow a "method." You sit down near the water. Child number one rushes right into the waves, loves it, and risks drowning if you aren't at hand. You keep having to haul him back from the deep water. Child two spends the vacation playing at the edge of the water. He shovels sand into it, watches it, and maybe at last splashes back and forth *after* you have put on his shoes to go home! You have allowed the youngster to be himself. You respect his individuality, and he in turn makes his very own relationship with that joy: a beach.

In the same way, we let the children come to our Lord by letting them know about him. We are careful to "go to the beach." We read an appropriate portion of God's word to them regularly. They can read his words, see that we are all in relationship with him, that we have a King, Savior, Helper, Friend. Later on, the *thinking* aspects—the realization that this is truth—will follow. But don't try to schedule *how* the child will feel, *how* he should react, *when* he should understand each step, etc. Get out of the way. Let the child, God, and his word be alone together. Let them work out their own relationship.

When I was three or four, a well-meaning adult troubled me no end. She said, "You should love Jesus more than you do your mummy and daddy." I was worried. In all honesty, I just knew I didn't. *Was I very, very wrong? Did God see that and mind?* I wondered.

Jesus lets little children remain who they are. He will meet them directly and will skillfully work into each separate life, telling them what is to be worked at, prayed about, and felt.

Teaching about the objective truth of Christianity is so very important that I will briefly apply the three "instruments of education" to this branch of the "curriculum."

The Atmosphere

Our children need to experience not intellectual assent to creeds only, but a day by day reality of those living life in relationship to a living King. The atmosphere of love, truth, humility, and forgiveness. The atmosphere of truly accepting the individual including his limitations. Accepting the gifts. The atmosphere of "hoping all things." The atmosphere of being open to the thoughts of our age. The atmosphere that everything matters and nothing is outside the reach of the light of God's truth.

The Discipline

Basically, we plan for the contact between child and truth; it is not left up to the chance moment. The Bible is read, and we pray together regularly, simply and with purpose. God hears, loves us, understands, and acts. We worship our King with other believers. We accept the responsibility (the routine) of serving each other. The acknowledgment of God's truth makes a practical difference in our schedules and priorities.

The Life

We let the child, from the first, have the objective source material: the Bible. We let him share with us as we worship. We do not exclude him from worries, questions, failures, or joys. We openly and honestly act like fellow human beings who are walking along the same road. Indeed, the child is, in many ways, to be our example. *He* is not to become like the grown-up church member. *We* are to become like the little child in our life with God. The reality of God's truth changes everything. It makes a difference to myself and to my relationship with everything that adds up to life.

> Let the little children come to me, and do not hinder them, for the kingdom of heaven belongs to such as these. (Mark 10:14)

Knowledge of Man: Putting a Child in Touch with the Human Race

History

> Perhaps the gravest defect in school curricula is that they fail to give a comprehensive, intelligent and interesting introduction to history. To leave off or even to begin with the history of our own country is fatal. We cannot live sanely unless we know that other peoples are as we are with a difference, that their history is as ours, with a difference, that they too have their literature and their national life.[7]

The Bible treats history seriously so that we may be put in touch with ordinary men and women who have gone before. We know what happens when certain absolutes are forgotten, when chaos reigns, or when tyranny takes over. Having known and having considered, we then are in a position to make more understanding judgments, choices. This is as true for us as individuals as it is for the communities we form.

I have heard that nobody can hope to be voted in as president of the USA if his or her TV personality isn't warm and beguiling. Where are the truly educated citizens who can direct the future of our countries by their wise choices? We don't seem to have people who have considered the consequence of wrong ideas. They seldom look to principles that are right, but rather to personal peace and affluence. They don't see themselves in a flow of history; they are isolated. They don't understand that all matters are interrelated.

It is never too late to mend but we may not delay to offer such a liberal and generous diet of History to every child in the country as shall give weight to his decisions, consideration to his actions and stability to his conduct; that stability, the lack of which has plunged us into many a stormy sea of unrest.[8]

Charlotte Mason once again understands the child, and she respects his own mind. We are exhorted to introduce the child to the living persons who peopled history, the episodes which are full of dramatic and emotional interest, and to the general consequence of the whole. In other words, we are *not* to use the teaching of history to communicate our own opinions or conclusions. Is it possible? Not perfectly. But our aim is honesty and knowledge of the truth.

In fact, it is important for the young person to know that there is a great deal to be said on both sides.

A small boy read a true story of a young German pilot who escaped from the British during the Second World War. His imagination was warmed by the spirit of this young man. He narrated the story to me, and at the end his eyes grew thoughtful. He was silent for a moment. Then, "I think this man was like a hero. He acted bravely. But he wasn't on the good side."

The child had come in touch with a deep reality. History isn't simple; we cannot reduce it to simple slogans. You can act with bravery and have real sincerity and yet be on the wrong side.

We err when we translate the past into our own terms. We should struggle for the truth. We should admit perplexities and look at the past honestly. This is a part of true academic excellence, of course.

It is a great thing to possess a pageant of history in the background of one's thoughts. We may not be able to recall this or that circumstance, but, "the imagination is warmed"; we know that there is a great deal to be said on both sides of every question and are saved from crudities in opinion and rashness in action. The present becomes enriched for us with the wealth of all that has gone before.[9]

First of all, we must ask why history is so often robbed of its value. It is often taught as a condensed summary of facts and dates. The mind rebels and is confused. Battles and treaties are muddled up from century to century.

A memory feat is *not* the first aim as we teach history. How do we awaken the child to the interest and fascination of this study?

We choose as accurate and well-written books as possible. Is the child too young to read a good literary history for himself? Then read to him aloud. Shun the babbling lecture. Let him get at the story itself; give him direct access to history.

This means that little history stories are not used. The child needs to be taught the consequences of events that happened in history. There is a flow to all of history, and none of it should be told in isolation.

The books should at first be so detailed that leisurely enjoyment of a whole period is possible. Charlotte Mason urges us to give the young child leisure to explore an age in detail. Choose a history of a period that actually introduces one to people who lived then, the great and the small. As much as possible, include source material. I feel I have met someone when I am able to read his own account, not merely what somebody else tells me about him. Let the tale live, flow. The child will breathe life into the past. His imagination will be touched, and he will bring judgment on it with his *own* mind. He will question, *Why? Was it right? What would have happened if . . . ?* and *What happened next?*

Again adults make the mistake of thinking children have to be twaddled at. Honey-sweet accounts turn off the ten-year-old just as much as anyone else.

Choose different kinds of history books. At first, do not trouble the child with what *you* want him to remember. Let him react himself. He may not remember the date of a treaty, but he may thrill with the ride of Paul Revere. He may remember the agonizing tug of war of conscience—"Which side shall I be on? King or revolution?"

As the narrative history story is read, one can add the reading of literary biographies that further bring alive an individual person or an era. Through the eyes of a real person, the atmosphere of a bygone age lives and breathes again. The child can identify with a human being, and then start to relate to what civil war, forms of government, etc., actually mean.

Charlotte Mason would not have us start with dry textbooks. Use readable, intelligent books that use intelligent language:

We can, at any rate, avoid giving children cut-and-dried opinions upon the course of history while they are yet young. What they want is graphic details concerning events and persons upon which the imagination goes to work; and opinions tend to form themselves by slow degrees as knowledge grows.[10]

The curriculum should be planned as a consecutive whole, so that as the child moves along, he gains a sense of the broad sweep of his own country's history and its place in the cultural history of the world. He will see how we are a world community and that we are not in isolation from one another. He will be able to see how beliefs have directed action.

We don't require a parrot-memorization of what he reads. Each time, Charlotte Mason would have us *listen* to the child as he accurately narrates what he has heard. This takes away the agony ("I can't remember that date!") and brings in personal interest and thinking. We are to help the child gain a sense of the time's flow. We take a good-sized sheet of art paper and divide it into a column for each century—so many BC and so many AD (which will bring us up to the present). As a historical narrative is read, one can then write down events and names in the appropriate century. Also, one can have a graphic portrayal of one century or period in this way. Divide a single century into decades, and watch what happened when. Another method, which younger children often much enjoy, is a scroll. After each history reading and its narration, the child then draws his own illustration of what happened. The next time history is read, he draws the next illustration. Use good paper and felt-tip pens. The child will cherish his own record, along with the book that has been a personal experience for him.

When such a child is older, he will enjoy quite an astonishing grasp of the flow of history, if the books have been wisely chosen. At this stage, he will have a rich groundwork, which will enable him to study for exams without mere cramming. He will be able to compare differing accounts. He will be increasingly able to relate other aspects of his study of man to the study of history. Novels will be read and seen against a particular historical background. Geography will be a consideration of places which affect people, and relationships will be grasped. Plays, poetry, religious expression, scientific discovery will all be read and related to the reality of the historical moment in which they were written. Biographies are to be pursued as are original essays, letters, and documents. Other aspects of human history will be seen in relationship to each other—art, music, architecture, governmental forms, laws, social and economic history.

In history, as in all educational life, we must make use of what actually surrounds us, as well as a sensitivity to the child's interest. A missionary mother who teaches her own children in India has told me how she makes full use of the richness of the local culture. As well as the hours spent in English "school," her five-year-old has grown to be fascinated with an interesting history book on India. This integrated education includes a meaningful friendship with an old village woman; the discussions in the vernacular would probably stimulate a Harvard student in oriental studies!

The child who has this door opened has an entry into the life story of the human race. He will never finish learning. Life is not long enough to fill the gaps.

Charlotte Mason urges us to take children to the places where things happened whenever possible. When there, they should not be pestered with little fact-sheets to fill in. They have been interested in the story first. Upon the ground of knowledge, the child will be able to react as he wants to. He will be able to stand and stare at one thing and ignore another. It will be *his*.

We will find, however, that the child, the person, thus educated by living history will not have to depend upon actually visiting a site to have the moment live and breathe.

In the PNEU schools at the end of a term, the child looked forward to the week when he could "tell" or write (essays) about any subject he had read. So for instance, a child might be asked, "Tell me all you can remember about the life of Florence Nightingale." The child would either dictate (if he was young) or write himself a long, factual, and detailed account of the story as it had stirred his imagination. The word-pictures and factual comments flowed. Several sides of paper might be covered. There was never any revision or cramming. The child was called upon to give out what he had heard, understood, enjoyed, and thought about.

This process illustrates to me what true education is all about.

Literature

Surely literature, books, and education all go hand in hand. From the earliest age, children delight in a good story. Indeed, it is hard to satisfy their appetite for stories. We must remember to separate the teaching of the reading *skill* from that of the place of true literature in the child's curriculum. I have already written of this principle at some length at the beginning of this book.

In literature, we have the opportunity of developing a series of relationships with other persons, places, and historical times in a direct way. Perhaps this is the best place for mind to meet mind. We all realize the deep influence our companions have upon our thinking and behavior. In literature, a child is introduced to persons who think deeply and sensitively and who express themselves well.

Why is literature central?

The object of children's literary studies is not to give them precise information as to who wrote what in the reign of whom?—but to give them a sense of the spaciousness of the days, not only of great Elizabeth, but of all those times of which poets, historians, and the makers of tales, have left us in living pictures. In such ways, the children secure, not the sort of information which is of little cultural value, but wide spaces wherein imagination may take those holiday excursions deprived of which life is dreary; judgment, too, will turn over these folios of the mind and arrive at fairly just decisions about a given strike, the question of Poland, Indian Unrest. Every man is called upon to be a statesman seeing that every man and woman, too, has a share in the government of the country; but statesmanship requires imaginative conceptions, formed upon pretty wide reading and some familiarity with historical precedents.[11]

Literature has a great natural power. Through it, we receive the gifted communication of other persons. In literature, perhaps more than through any other art form, we are able to get into the other man's shoes.

A family, a class, or any group that reads aloud has a sense of communion as they share together ideas and human experiences. TV is not a substitute for literature. It has displaced books in many families, but literary education is a priority to consider.

Last week my daughter was in a college English class, and she mentioned that our family reads together almost every evening. The reaction was electric. The students were amazed. "Where do you read?" (Do families no longer have *living* rooms?) "What could you all share?" (*A Tale of Two Cities.*) "Your *dad* reads aloud? You *all* listen?" (Yes, ages eleven to forty-five listening together.) It seems sad to me that this struck the class and its teacher as almost unbelievable. (One girl remarked, "Why, you could write a book about your family!")

The Bible is literature as well as history and truth about God and man. In the 1930s, my father knew simple folk who had never had an "education." They still lived in simple cabins in the southern states of America. For the oldest ones, slavery was still a fairly recent memory. But Dad said that some of these persons were truly educated people in the true and wide sense. Why? They had read the Bible. The wholeness of this Book had educated them.

Children must not think that "readers" are the only books. How they love fairy tales, fables, myths! They love the ancient heroic tales. Don't look for twaddle on "their level." Charlotte Mason found that even deprived children responded to really good literature. By the age of nine, ten, or eleven, they were ready to appreciate the reading of Shakespeare's plays. Did they understand every bit?

We spread an abundant and delicate feast in the programmes and each small guest assimilates what he can. The child of genius and imagination gets greatly more than his duller comrade but all sit down to the same feast and each one gets according to his needs and powers.[12]

How do I "spread the feast"? Some children devour books. But there are more who shun them. The secret lies in enjoying them together: one reads aloud expressively.

I once cared for an emotionally deprived child. She couldn't concentrate; her eyes flitted here and there. At that time, we were reading *The Lion, the Witch and the Wardrobe* by C. S. Lewis to our own children. One night by the fireside, the story grabbed her. Her body relaxed. She listened, enthralled. "Please read more," she begged with the others.

Is reading aloud only for little ones? A college teacher told me once that his students couldn't enjoy Shakespeare or even the Brontës. What about reading *aloud*? Many are strangers to the joy of literature. The feast needs spreading.

One of the duties of those guiding the education of children, young people, and indeed persons of any age at all is to choose good books. Literature is the human heart of education.

There is, however, one very real problem. Though it was one that Charlotte Mason faced in some measure in the 1920s, it is far more acute today.

Children are faced all too soon with the cruel reality of the fallen world. There is sin and suffering. The parent's responsibility is a delicate balance. On the one hand, the young should not be dragged through horrifying and evil places. On the other hand, we should not shield them totally from the world the way it is.

What then do we do about literature which is anything but pure, lovely, of good report (Phil. 4:8)?

The twenty-first century abounds in the cynical, the immoral, the ugly. Love and loyalty are often spoken of as sentimental.

This is a difficult problem. We have to work out the solution in different ways for different individuals and situations. However, we should not, at any age, allow ourselves to be totally immersed in the negative, nonhuman, amoral, or immoral perspective.

I believe that young children get quite enough of the abnormal world as they actually live in it, and they hear plenty of conversations about its effects too. I personally think that the harm in TV portrayals of the sordid, frightening, and violent lies in the fact that it is at the same time *too real* and yet *not real enough*. A small child is more immediately involved in the death of a bird, say, than in five deaths on TV. But TV leaves images which should not be there. The child has enough of sin and failure, cruelty and problems in real life.

If the child is given a diet of literature in "good books," he learns to "feel" with all sorts of persons. He will think about and judge incidents on the basis of what he realizes is right. Although protected by the literary form, he can read about a wide variety of human experiences, including sin, disappointment, tragedy, despair.

If we begin by choosing the tried and true, the *best* of literature, we will give the child a love of excellence and the really "good." As we go on reading he will find that there are distressing happenings, stories which need discussion. Literature can help children think about what life is like before they live it as adults.

At some teenage stage, the young person should also read and appreciate good secular twenty-first-century adult literature. He needs to understand where our culture is, why the questions are so acute, and how lost and desperate so many people feel today. The Christian parent, friend, or teacher should also read these books; not to give lectures on them, but so that they can enjoy a valuable art form and discuss relevant ideas together. It helps these older children to understand *why* some people write like this, *what* they think about the human being, God, morality, society.

A child has to be put in touch with his own age and not just the world of long ago (which, incidentally, was also sinful and fallen). However, this "putting in touch" shouldn't turn into the total influence at any one time. As I said before, I think the balance has to be sought individually from the Lord. "If any of you lacks wisdom, he should ask God, who gives generously . . ." (James 1:5).

Pray for wisdom. We live in a decadent generation. Be prepared to make mistakes and to learn from them.

The PNEU curriculum introduced a study of the history of English literature when the students were about thirteen years old. A book that was interesting to read was used, and the period studied in any one semester corresponded with the period the students were covering in history.

Literature is an important and central part of education. Make sure that the habit of reading is established. Make time for reading at home and at school. It is the base of education.

Morals and Citizenship

By this stage, you will have realized that Charlotte Mason's approach was to relate the child to the past, to ideas, and to "subjects" by reading to him and later having him read books which were "living" rather than factual recitations or outlines. In addition, however, the PNEU syllabus singled out the need for the child to be given material specifically designed to cover the subjects of morals, economics, and citizenship.

She used as a foundation North's *Lives of the Greeks and Romans*. This was read aloud by the teacher, and it drew the child into the life of those working and living in the ancient world. As in any such history of human endeavor, there were failures, sins, and weaknesses displayed as well as responsible, good, and heroic action. But the text made no comment about which was right or wrong. Charlotte Mason, however, did advise the teacher to make "certain omissions" (presumably of passages illustrating certain specific sexual or other sins).

She found that the children began to show a sympathetic understanding of the problems of statesmanship, and they would put themselves in Pericles's shoes—for instance, when asked to narrate, "How did Pericles manage the people in time of war lest they should force him to act against his own judgment?"

When a ten-year-old can answer that with a fluent narration, he has the chance of working out for himself the ideas and principles involved, and the practical difficulties of integrating them into society.

The secret of effective teaching lies in gaining the child's interest and sympathy. Later on, he will then see the need of organized government and will be ready to be taught about the administrative structure of his own country and international relationships. Intertwined with citizenship is morals. After all, that is why the state must have laws. The Supreme Court is important, but in a sense the individual's ideas about law are a more powerful influence in society.

This is one area where I believe we are in a very different place from Charlotte Mason. Our generation's most vocal communicators in society in general are preaching a non-Christian, post-Christian, or humanist base to law (morality, citizenship). Therefore, children experience a form of brainwashing. This is one important reason why some responsible parents have come to the conclusion that their children are not managing to stay "free" as they go through the typical secular school network. That would worry me too. There is no such thing as a neutral teacher. Every teacher does influence the child. The books used too may have been written with a specific "hook." For instance, check out the sex education material. It may actually encourage wrong behavior (wrong from the Christian viewpoint)—sin. We therefore have the frightening possibility that children may be denied Christian references yet be bombarded with a calculated attempt to shape their basic moral thinking.

The priorities we have looked at, including those of relating the child to the teaching about (and from) God, about history, and about literature may be achieved in many ways, very successfully. Child A comes from a Christian home and attends the secular school down the road. It is a "good school" and serves the child reasonably well. The parents spend lots of time with the child, giving him a full life shared with them. So his "center of gravity" is his home. There he listens to the Bible being read, gets to discuss ideas, and the family reads aloud together regularly every evening. This reading fills gaps and puts the child in touch with literature, etc. The children enjoy the richness of people, nature, and relaxation with the parents. Their church is a community, and this too is a "center of gravity" in the children's lives.

These children enjoy their friends and have time to invent their own play and creative activities. They actually benefit from mixing regularly with "ordinary" people every day at school. Instead of just hearing that "some people don't think that God made the world," they listen to Mr. Smith actually teaching that point of view. They may challenge him, and they will certainly come home ready to discuss his viewpoint. It won't be theoretical, but they will relate it to actual situations. Child A's parents assume responsibility for the child, and they are able to fulfill, reasonably adequately, some or many of the above needs in their child's life.

The children in family B are in a different position. They may go off to the same school. However, at home both parents are pressed for time, due to career, community, and/or church commitments.

They are unable to complete the picture at home. The children are picking up more and more of the secular pattern of mind. Perhaps, since the family lacks a "center of gravity" of life, the children are swept up by the peer group. Morally, they are pushed into behavior which is downright destructive and/or wrong, from the Christian viewpoint. Children are very different from each other. Some "cross over the line" with more or less pressure on either side of the fence. Maybe in family A there is a child who is as influenced by the secular school environment as a child in family B and vice versa.

The reasons why may differ. But in case B, the child will be sucked under by a tide that is flowing too hard for him. It is our duty to remove him from the riptide and put his little boat into calmer waters, while he develops maturity, thinking, and everything I have been writing about as education.

These "calmer waters" may be provided by changes made in the family life of family B. They may choose new priorities. Or, even following such a plan, it may still be right to also alter the school influence by providing a different daily environment. Really good schools are needed for the child whose home cannot provide for his needs in a basic area. We must realize that there are increasing numbers of such homes or situations (such as a single parent struggling to be both breadwinner *and* 100 percent of the family's servant/shepherd). Any family may welcome the active good such a school will do for the child in the totality of his life. Indeed, it may be the child's only hope, a real lifeline.

All persons interested in moral teaching must consider the influence of the media. It is sobering to think that deep moral attitudes, including the way in which social responsibility is regarded, is absorbed through a child's very pores from the atmosphere surrounding him day by day. Is the home strong enough?

Is there enough well-rounded life to give a "center of gravity" away from the current secular society? Watch out! These aren't words on paper. A person's *life* is at stake.

In developing a moral and responsible sense, the child *must* have the possibility of discussing, verbalizing, and judging for himself. This is, as I see it, one of the valuable insights Charlotte Mason leaves with us as she described this branch of education.

She chose Plutarch's *Lives* for several reasons. But here is an aspect to consider (although we might have to look for another book to teach the same things to today's child):

Now Plutarch is like the Bible in this, that he does not label the actions of his people as good or bad but leaves the conscience and judgment of his readers to make that classification. What to avoid and how to avoid it, is knowledge as important to the citizen whether of the City of God or of his own immediate city, as to know how to perform the same. Children recognise with incipient weariness the doctored tale as soon as it is begun to be told, but the human story with its evil and its good never flags in interest. . . .

Perhaps we are so made that the heroic which is all heroic, the good which is all virtuous, palls upon us, whereas we preach little sermons to ourselves on the text of the failings and weaknesses of those great ones with whom we become acquainted in our reading. Children, like ourselves, must see life whole if they are to profit.[13]

Therefore, as we ourselves focus on the moral issues in literature, history, etc., we will ensure that children are nurtured on books which open the door to their understanding in these areas. We do not preach or moralize. If they are growing up surrounded by those who *practice* God's morality, they themselves will think and express judgments using their own minds. Remember that these children are in daily contact with the rule book, God's word. We can do no better.

We have to look long and hard at the individual child, our home, school, and outside influences. Just because a home or school is "Christian" does not mean that the child is being properly helped, grounded, educated as a whole person. We accept that nothing is perfect, but we try to get our priorities right. We are ready to take time and trouble to see that our children aren't swept off in a roaring tide. But we want more than that. We pray for a person who is like the individual mentioned in Psalm 1. He has grown like an oak tree by a stream. Storms may roar, a branch or two may snap, but the oak stands firmly grounded—so much so that small creatures seek shelter therein.

There is no one method to achieve such a mature person. There is no perfect or complete situation. We must pray for the individual, pray for wisdom, open our eyes, choose priorities. We must not only talk. We have to serve, give, and be willing to live with the children. We nurture with *life*.

Composition

According to Charlotte Mason's educational principles and practice, the various subjects are interrelated. In fact, she believed that in teaching "composition," teachers and schools often got in the way of the child's development. However, the PNEU-educated child was encouraged to respond to each subject with a narration, a telling. Charlotte Mason was aware of the powerful growth this gave the child in verbal skills—first oral and later written.

... The art of composition, that art of "telling" which culminates in a Scott or a Homer and begins with the toddling persons of two and three who talk a great deal to each other and are surely engaged in a "telling" ... But children of six can tell to amazing purpose. The grown-up who writes the tale of their "telling" will cover many pages, before getting to the end of "Hansel and Gretel" or "The Little Match Girl" or a Bible story. The facts are sure to be accurate and the expression surprisingly vigorous, striking and unhesitating. Probably few grownups could "tell" one of Aesop's Fables with the terse directness which children reproduce.[14]

So Charlotte Mason opens the door to natural, individual, creative development of language. It involves the child's thinking.

To begin with, a small child tells back the stories he has heard. If he has a good grounding in the mechanical skills of writing, Charlotte Mason considered the child able to use his own writing to give back the narration by the time he was about nine years old. It was always based on reading which had interested him. She had the startlingly progressive view that such early writing should not be hindered by worry about detail (spelling, punctuation, etc.). That skill can be worked on separately.

After all, by the time they reached nine years of age, they would have had three years of narrating on a wide variety of subjects. They would be quite experienced. They would also have had three years to learn spelling and writing as a skill. At some moment, the child is ready to translate his advanced narration skill into the harder skill of transcribing his own thoughts and expressions in writing. The changeover is not made all at once. It will be at a different age for different children. Some learn the technical skills of writing faster than others.

Another powerful factor in this approach is that the child has had a daily diet of books written by persons of well-above-average abilities of communication. They are deeply influenced by the ideas, standard, and breadth of expression in such nurturing. If the teacher follows Charlotte Mason's principles, she won't get in the way:

> As the object of every writer is to explain himself in his own book, the child and the author must be trusted together, without the intervention of the middle-man. What his author does not tell him he must go without knowing for the present. No explanation will really help him, and explanations of words and phrases spoil the text and should not be attempted unless children ask, What does so and so mean? when other children in the class will probably tell.[15]

Thus, the child is nurtured, in a sense, not by the teacher at all. He is allowed to interact with especially gifted and varied persons. He responds and grows in a sort of personal dialogue suited for his own self. He will be able to respond and expand in all sorts of expressions. For example, Charlotte Mason found that children created wonderful poetry.

There is another bonus. The PNEU child, thus occupied, actually came to *know* the curriculum he was responding to. It was inwardly digested. He would relate it to his personal life, culture, and to other subjects.

Literary expression is a basic product of education, as well as being the means provided by God for creative communication, appreciation and reaction, and a mark of our individuality. It must be encouraged, allowed, practiced.

Start by *listening*. Take time to listen (it even works with grown-ups!).

Some children spend their days in reasonably useful schools which never provide for this growth. In many English schools, classes have up to thirty-eight children! How can one adult listen to them all? She can't. Can even twenty be listened to?

Could volunteer mothers come in to read to a small group and listen to the telling back? Could one disruptive and antisocial child be taken to a cozy spot, and be alone to talk with a sympathetic adult every day? I believe many grandmothers and grandfathers would provide their human warmth and interest if the problem was explained to them. Such a child is crying out for attention. The child could then tell back the story and watch his very own words being written down. No audio recording or computer can do this. By it, several needs are met.

Parents should realize how much they can do at home when the school cannot educate or is not educating the child in this area. As well as reading, listen and encourage the telling back. When an older child reads a book for himself, casually ask for the story. Try this when driving; switch off the car radio. A teenager too should "tell." In a relationship, such narration is a kind of giving from the child. If it is appreciated, the child will glow with personal satisfaction.

"That was interesting."

"You certainly grasped that book well."

"Thank you. Now I understand Camus better. I think I'd like to read that book, too."

Regular family meals should be times of telling. We need to move from the important telling of the day's happenings to the sharing of books read, plays seen, etc.

Children enjoy good quality notebooks in which to write. Again, time has to be unhurried and TV-free if such gentle arts are to be encouraged.

Another natural area for writing in the family is letters. First, let the child receive letters. If they go away to camp, for instance, communicate in an interesting way. Encourage letter writing (and practice it). A letter is a gift. When children pass the "I am fine. How are you? My cat died. I am learning to swim" stage, they will start to be able to *share* in writing, as it is their habit already in speaking. Children should not write contrived letters. Letters to mail-order toy firms or other letters to businesses, for example, should be written and actually mailed. Keep a carbon, and paste it and the reply in a notebook. Letters to absent friends and relatives also help to develop this sense of communication with the "real world."

There may be a big stumbling-block in that the child may not have acquired the basic writing and spelling skills. Maybe he has been turned off by bad experiences. Do something about it! Have the child examined by a specialist to find out whether there is some reason, such as a dyslexic tendency. Expert advice may be needed.

Make it a priority to fill this gap in his education. Being able to express oneself well and clearly is too important to leave to chance development. Daily structured practice is necessary in such cases. But it shouldn't take the place of play. I have found that such problems are best tackled as one of the first priorities of the morning. A regular ten- or fifteen-minute slot of one-to-one work can result in good progress. Success should be built in; the steps should be appropriate. There are good materials based on a multisensory approach. It is up to us to find ways that will work with a given child. But remember the friendly atmosphere. The child may be feeling a terrible failure, "dumb," or "bad." Love will encourage another attempt. "I can't" can turn into "I can." This is most likely when, after the regular lesson, the child isn't forced to struggle over this mechanical skill for long periods of time. For him, the richness and relaxation of the rest of the day will help keep him fresh for the effort, while encouraging general growth, interest, and confidence.

Families, schools, life—all work either to educate or to "clam up" the child as a person who understands and who has the power of expression.

Languages

If we are to pursue Charlotte Mason's philosophy of education, we see that we are engaged in introducing the child to his possible relationships with other persons in the past, and with those who live in other places. For a direct experience of the latter, it is especially helpful to learn at least one other language. To be introduced to another language is to have an insular barrier removed. Different expression and ideas in words challenge the inward-looking tendency. It is part of a liberal education.

But Charlotte Mason would have us *really* teach the language so that it can be spoken, enjoyed, be a part of life. This is a challenge, indeed!

It used to be that the educated child was grounded in Latin, and maybe Greek. Such a child gained some sense of the flow of history and the development of language. We may or may not think that our own child would benefit from learning a classical language. But it is well worth considering the advantages of learning a modern one.

Charlotte Mason applied her general principles of education in this area as well. She advocated that fluency in a spoken language (say, French) should be gained before the written grammar was tackled. She advised that about six new words be introduced daily. The spoken vocabulary and language power would slowly be built up. The child should hear a simple French phrase (or a poem, song, narration, etc.), and then repeat it back. This was found to work better than memorization.

It is well known that young children can pick up a second language orally. To achieve this, the language has to be allowed to escape from the lesson and become part of everyday life. Charlotte Mason had slightly older pupils act out French fables. Then, too, there was a regular nature walk when everybody would speak French.

Later on, as with their own language, children would proceed from speaking to reading French books. Last came the formal grammar. Students thus taught were able as teenagers to listen to a half-hour lecture on Molière, and talk or write about it accurately and with understanding. When Charlotte Mason tells us that these ordinary youngsters had the same facility in German, and even Italian, one's envy grows, especially when one remembers that they had also been afforded the grounding of Latin and sometimes Greek!

It is amazing to us who have experienced mediocre education to think that quite ordinary boys and girls are capable of such growth. And these are children who have *not* been pressured with an ambitious program. They were the ones who started out with only ten minutes of writing at six and seven so that they wouldn't become restless and tired. They weren't given homework, and had free afternoons and evenings for generous leisure in and out of doors. How was this achieved? Is it an unattainable ideal? No.

Many schools excel in wasting time. Time is like a fortune; it is wrong to allow it to be buried. Children are tired out with busy work. They are talked at until their attention habitually wanders, and maybe nine-tenths of their time is wasted. There are many children who don't even know their own language, let alone anyone else's!

There is one other problem in language education. The child should have someone who actually *knows* the language teach him. Again, modern audiovisual material is especially helpful in language teaching, but the child needs contact with someone who can *talk* and *listen*. They need the personal touch. Such teachers are not always easily found. It may be hard to locate a teacher who is fluent in the language, but this should be the aim.

This is one of the many areas where a missionary's children taught at home will be at a tremendous advantage. They have many natural relationships in at least one second language. Children are superb linguists.

Knowing at least one second language is not as necessary as being liberally educated in one's own language. But it is a door that should be opened, if possible. It is not really a luxury; it is part of our human growth.

Art

It is lovely to observe a small child experimenting with pots of paint. Children spontaneously express themselves in painting and drawing. One necessary and primary provision, therefore, is to make good materials available to the child at home and at school. Art is one of the basics for little children. They love talking, listening to stories, and drawing or painting.

Charlotte Mason, however, did not isolate the child within his own expression. Just as she led the child directly to the best books she could find, so she led the child to great art.

In the PNEU school, the year had three terms. Each term the child was given his personal envelope containing six reproductions of works by a single artist. When my children were in a PNEU school, Rembrandt, Millet, Picasso, and countless others became known.

The child is given his first reproduction. He looks at it, and you let him talk about the picture. You don't lecture about schools of painting or style. The child is allowed direct and fresh access to the picture itself. At first, he may focus on little. Maybe his eyes are glazed by TV watching. Maybe everything is a sort of visual fog. When the child has had a chance to look to his heart's content, turn the picture face downwards, and get him to describe what he saw. "There was a beach, with a wrecked ship. I think it was going to rain. One of the fishermen had bare feet. There was a village on the hill." He then turns it over and with interest checks the picture again.

Next time, the skill will become sharper, the child more observant. He will regard the pictures as friends. Make it a happy warm time, just like when you enjoy a story together.

The PNEU child was also given a blank piece of paper to sketch roughly what he remembered of the picture. I was amazed at the delicately accurate and sensitive results children achieved. Of course, as with the narration, children are offering something of themselves. We must not jump on it critically: "You're wrong, you made the house bigger than it was." We must let them see for themselves. They then turn the picture over and look at it *hard*. Maybe they'll want to try again.

Children whose minds and spirits are nourished with these paintings will, in turn, look at the world around them with new eyes. They will comment on the quality of dappled light under the trees, or note that the storm clouds remind them of a Rembrandt landscape. It is a wealth that will remain with them for life. Let a six-year-old have his very own art book after he has spent three months on a particular artist. He'll probably still cherish it when he is forty! It's special when children can "find" their own originals in a museum. Mine always charged through the National Gallery in London with great excitement.

"Mommy, where is *my* painting?"

Then a long appreciative pause, and a deep sigh of satisfaction. "Oh, *there's* my painting. It's bigger and better than I thought."

Words fail the child. He stands in deep contemplation. Don't hurry him off! Don't try to get him to "see everything." You'll give him pictorial indigestion. One sure way of making a person hate apples is to take him to an orchard at 9:00 a.m. and force-feed him apples until noon! Indeed, the revulsion may last a lifetime. So it is with pictures and museums.

Later on, a child with this rich background will find it interesting to relate art to history, literature, and culture. Time enough later for an understanding of schools, styles, development. Charlotte Mason included exposure to architecture, as an artistic expression, in the same way.

Children thus nurtured will continue to paint and draw their own original pictures. They will not be intimidated by Dürer if they aren't foolishly encouraged to copy his work. The memory-picture was not a copy. It was a kind of graphic narration.

Also, let the children illustrate a story that has interested them. They should have good-quality notebooks with good pencils, etc. How they love to "see" with the eyes of their own imagination and record their seeing! Children become discouraged by their lack of expertise if they are used to "coloring in" an adult's outline.

I think that Sunday schools too should stay away from such prepared (and boring) papers to color in. How about large sheets of good-quality paper and felt-tip pens for younger children, and drawing pencils for older children? If their emotion and interest has been stirred by the story, their visual record will be a personal expression or creation and contribute to their *knowing*. It is beautiful to see Peter's astonishment as he finds himself outside of the prison gate, the fear of the Jewish family as the plagues of Egypt approach their homes, etc., through the imaginative pictures of a child.

As well as drawing pictures stimulated by stories, children in the PNEU school were encouraged to respond to nature. I'll describe their nature notebooks later, but they would bring back a flower or other find and paint it in watercolor. The first attempts were rough, but slowly the child responded to the individuality and beauty of what he found and brought back. The record was treasured. This is another "related art." The child's seeing eye is opened to the fragile and special world of creation.

Charlotte Mason leaves us challenged to encourage creativity in many ways, by many means. It brings all sorts of benefits and largeness of spirit (magnanimity) to the child. The child who has to live in sordid urban surroundings may find this of special value. Open windows to beautiful scenes through art! Try it with a child from the inner city. Can you open the closed door a little crack? Offer a wide variety of artistic expression. Children enjoy clay modeling and other artistic handicrafts.

Art and creativity should be encouraged at home as well as at school. Money has to be spent on the materials, and you have to ignore the mess that some art activity means. As with anything else, why don't the grown-ups try their hands at painting and drawing, too? The atmosphere produced is calm, friendly, satisfying, and purposeful. Winston Churchill and many people operating under great strain found this was a true recreation.

When the children were small, we used to pack a "quiet bag" for vacations. After a tiring morning on the beach, we would drive to a shady green hill, with satisfying views of sea, coves, and valleys. Mother and Dad each painted, right along with any child who wanted to. There were other quiet occupations to choose from, but our sketches remain treasured memories. Today one of those pictures can bring back the whole "feel" of the day.

Music

Say "music" and "children" in the same breath, and you might think of children reluctantly practicing the piano. The discipline of learning a musical instrument provides the foundation for enjoyment and creativity later on. Today there are several good methods of teaching music, for example the Suzuki method. It is a worthwhile enterprise. Think of the benefits to both the individual and to the group when someone can play or sing. There is always special joy in group singing; music is part of our human response, creativity, and enjoyment of beauty.

Even before an instrument is tackled we will, if we follow Charlotte Mason's principles, have music be part of the life and atmosphere surrounding the young child. And, as I have said elsewhere in this book, it should be good music. Just as children begin their literary education sitting on their parent's knee, so even a baby will respond to music while relaxing with the family. How about Beethoven's *Fifth* every Saturday morning as the children hop into their parents' bed for a special cuddle?

In the PNEU school, just as in each third of the school year the child came to know the paintings of one artist, so they would be put in touch with one composer. In three school years (first through third grade), a child would have come to know some music by nine different composers!

Perhaps one week, say Tuesday, the children would enjoy an art reproduction, talk about it, sketch it from memory, etc. The following Tuesday, they might listen to part of a Bach chorale or a Beethoven symphony. At first one plays a short, catchy part of the whole work. It should not be a lesson, long and serious, which makes children squirm! Or how about playing the different parts of the symphony after lunch while the children rest for fifteen minutes? There would be various ways of working it in, but the love of the richness of this part of human expression should not be degraded to a monstrous blaring diet of current music. I think that families, schools, and groups should consciously foster richness of musical enjoyment. Support concerts and choral singing (both doing it and going to listen). Grown-ups might go to a local college so that they can take a music appreciation class to expand their own enjoyment. We need to open doors for ourselves so that fresh breezes blow into our lives.

Music should be a part of life at many levels. If it is, children will inherit this part of the human legacy. Let it not be cheap, narrow, or shallow.

One offshoot of musical life will be musical creativity. Small children chant their very own songs. Others, learning to play the piano, will begin to experiment with chords. Those learning, say, the recorder, would like to improvise along with a Purcell or Bach recording of chamber music. Put out percussion instruments; encourage the young to accompany recordings. Accept and admire the products. Let them perform for you. Organize a musical evening with friends. Serve a buffet supper, and then let the children and adults perform. Even the preschool child will delight in singing, "Twinkle, Twinkle, Little Star."

When there is music, the child responds with dancing. Even a ten-month-old infant who has learned to walk early will dance like a funny little clown! This is very good. Some music encourages dancing more than others! I'll never forget a wet, dull, and dark suppertime when I was about three years old. The radio suddenly burst out with a cheerful tune. A delighted self watched my slim, aproned young mother suddenly whirl, clap, and waltz to the music. The rush of happiness was so vivid I recall it still. From then on, Mommy seemed somehow a more cheerful, zestful, fun person to me. Children thrive on the atmosphere of joyous good music, feeling free to dance and sing and skip.

We have found that our family and friends have enjoyed the social aspect of square dancing, English country dances, and Scottish dancing. This gives a happy spice to community life, and it's nice to see six-year-olds mixing happily with mature adults in fun. Teenagers join in, and we are all people together, not segregated into age groups.

Schools will find that "music and movement" sessions relax the children. Many girls love doing dance instead of eternal physical jerks and exercises.

Although music in worship is not part of our discussion in this chapter, one thing must be said. There has been a growing tendency to supplant the musically rich heritage of the Christian church with endless monotonous choruses. Some of the lighter Christian music makes enjoyable singing; some is of good quality and merits a place in the repertoire. But one of the human responses in our relationship with God has always been a musical response. Surely, this should also be dignified, rich, and of a good musical standard.

Music! Into the drab and hurried blur of breathless twenty-first-century life, allow time and enjoyment and growth for this aspect of our humanness. It is part of a liberal education.

Knowledge of the Universe: Putting a Child in Touch with His Planet

Science

Why teach science?

So the child can enjoy and understand his relationship with the world and universe he lives in. So that he can say, "I feel at home here, I belong; I understand, appreciate, know."

In the past fifty years, the sheer volume of scientific knowledge has built up to include vast quantities of detail. How can we tackle it in school (or at home)?

The Christian begins by accepting a particular perspective. We are talking about the nature of the creation of our God: we are observing *his* handiwork. And it is spine-chillingly wonderful. There is no greater obstacle to an enjoyment and understanding of these vistas than too technical an approach.

Charlotte Mason advised us to involve children directly with the world, letting them enjoy, wonder, and question themselves. She included direct observation and accurate recording from the earliest age. At the same time, she would have us hunt for "treasure"—books which open up the wonder and excitement of the created world.

Families following Charlotte Mason's home education books would have started off by giving the young child ample time to play in the great outdoors every day. If the child was unable to run out of the kitchen door to play in a garden, Charlotte Mason advised the young urban mother to make this a priority. She would have us pack up essentials and get the children out to woods or meadow one afternoon a week (at least). There the parent sits down and plunks baby on the grass while the older children rush off with cries of delight to explore the area. Nature is a great teacher! Children wonder, look, ask, climb. When the children are tired of the first rush, Charlotte Mason has a good idea. She would have us say, "Why don't you climb that little hill, and look at what is over it? Then come back and describe to me what you have seen." The children rush off and come running back, full of descriptions of what they have noticed. Another idea is to verbalize views.

"Oh, how I love the line of these hills. Let's look hard and see it like a picture. We'll close our eyes and try to 'look' from memory. Then, anytime in life when we need it, we can open a window and see these hills in the autumn sunshine!"

Another of her ideas, which children love, is to adopt trees in a patch of woods. Susie may have an old oak tree, Billy has a maple, and so on. When they come to "their" woods, they'll run to their own trees. This way, they become intimate with the names of trees without suffering lectures and memorization!

In our own family, when we lived on the outskirts of London, we developed a similar pattern ourselves. We didn't own a car, so baby, diapers, and food would all be packed into a backpack or two. The older children and ourselves would make our way to a bus stop, and we would be whizzed away from urban sprawl into living, breathing countryside. The West of London merges into a lovely area that reminds me of Pennsylvania. In fact, we would hike through Penn's Woods, past the villages that Penn had come from!

The children and ourselves looked forward all week to our day-off walk. And they really learned to walk! (One three-year-old was capable of a steady six miles, taken slowly over a day, with lots of rest-and-refreshment stops.) Nature is God's gift to us, an environment created for us. It is well worth making this a top priority.

In the PNEU school, all children went out for a nature walk one afternoon a week, the six- to eighteen-year-olds included! Charlotte Mason advises us that this should be especially striven for in the case of urban children whose daily lives are cut off from nature. TV has often given children and adults the false illusion that they have really seen something because they have seen it on the box. Take the ocean. A child may watch a program on tides and waves. But his true scientific interest and understanding will not be like that of the child who has explored and lived on a beach for a couple of weeks.

As in other areas, Charlotte Mason tells us not to get in the child's way. The walk should not be a nature lecture. The child will pick a flower and ask, "What is this flower called?" Our challenge, as adults, is to know the names ourselves! Such walks are leisurely; there must be time to look at the ants crawling over the path, time to throw stones in the stream, and then float twigs down. Be ready to name, explain, share, listen, and wonder.

We should not always take children to places which they have not been before. By going back to the same place, as the seasons change, they notice changes, they observe in-depth. These PNEU children would bring back their own specimens from the walk. Maybe a fungus lugged proudly by a small boy, or leaves, bark, a snail, a flower. Each child has his own nature notebook in which to paint whatever he brought back and then write his own description. If possible, it is good for the teacher (or parent) to keep a nature notebook too; it is a life we live together. Often on such walks, it will be the children who challenge you. "How interesting. I really don't know the answer to that. I'll try to find a book in the library that will tell us." The nature specimens could be displayed on a table, neatly labeled for all to look at.

Children nurtured in this way are appreciative and observant. They learn to name the environment they live in. Birds, flowers, insects, rocks—all come into focus.

Of course, this experience relates to the study of geography as well as science. Charlotte Mason urges us to set special observation tasks for older children.

"We'll make a chart of the temperature in the garden, the woods, and by the lake."

"Where is the sun first thing in the morning? At noon? In the late afternoon?"

They should go outside to *look* north, south, east, and west. They should see how sun and stars relate to these directions. They'll enjoy noticing cloud formation, wind velocity, pond water seen through a microscope, etc., etc. There is a lot of excellent educational science project work available. But Charlotte Mason reminds us that the groundwork comes from the child living and seeing, experiencing and touching. For this reason, I would never use a canned visual sequence on nature for the under-eight-year-old. They must, as much as possible, have *direct contact*.

Of course, Charlotte Mason saw that this logically led the child on to laboratory experimentation and recording.

Yet she sees a parallel line of learning. These children are having direct personal contact with the material of the world. This has its limitations because each child and adult is very limited in his personal experience. Therefore, she would have us introduce science books that are really interesting to read. For younger children this means reading aloud to them. They will be fascinated. Some will be passionately hooked. They can then begin to explore, in a leisurely fashion, the fascinating makeup of all that is around them. She advises us to choose books that will fall into an ordered sequence. Children should first be drawn into understanding the things they have experienced firsthand. What are clouds? Where does the water go in the rivers? Why do seeds sprout? A dry answer does not woo interest. Look for books that "tell" in an interesting way, so that the child can narrate back to you the "story."

She warns us not to burden them with huge lists of facts to memorize. Think how much scientific knowledge, words, and concepts are built up "by the way" in the child of one to six years! In the same way, these children will build up an amazing understanding and interest in the world around them through *direct* contact and through carefully chosen reading.

By the time such a child is ready for more advanced and specific scientific study, his mind will be interested, noticing, thinking. He will feel at home in the universe and in his own world. He will realize that there are some questions that nobody yet knows the answer to, and some of these have been guessed at with a theoretical answer. Even the young child will have noticed the difference between the Genesis account of creation and the "normal" scientific explanation of beginnings. It is good that when this question is brought up, an explanation is given of the fact that as some people do not believe in God, they can't really explain how things started at all. They should be aware of the fact that evolution is a theory (an educated guess). It is *not* science versus the Bible.

Later on, children should have access to accurate scientific material which explains the strong and the weak points of evolutionary theory. They should get an inside peek at the disagreements among scientists.

One should not make the study of evolution more central than it should be. These and other philosophical, ethical, and moral questions will arise out of scientific study. As in other areas, we should be able to discuss the *relationship* of biblical truth to current cultural belief (which is more an issue here than the scientific study under which it enters).

A child will advance to more specific scientific study. We need to keep a few of Charlotte Mason's educational principles in mind.

Some children will never go on to advanced work in the sciences. Do our course plans cater to his need of understanding, knowledge, skill, while not removing the wonder and beauty of the subjects? I heard a nuclear physicist who said that in his field he was constantly excited and awed by the sheer wonder of what he pursued. Is there no way we could combine the more structured learning with a sense of wonder, questioning, awe? This is a challenge in science teaching. It should be accurate and good, leaving the person with a sure grasp of reality so that he is more likely to think for himself and not to feel vulnerable and weak when the "experts" pontificate. He should know that the ordinary citizen need not hand over decisions to "the experts" as if he had no mind or responsibility. I believe that this is vital in the coming generation. We can easily be intimidated by experts. Let the children know enough so that they will think for themselves.

Other teenagers will obviously benefit from a full study of all the scientific branches so as to prepare them for entry into various professions and industry. This teaching should be good, expert, advanced. However, such students should always be encouraged to relate their studies to the ideas in the other branches of knowledge of God and man. The study of science should not be allowed to be conducted in isolation from life. We desperately need scientists who do not lose contact with reality or with the Christian framework and its implications. I think that young science students would benefit from discussions with persons who hold different points of view. They also need to be able to discuss with (not be lectured at by) practicing Christian experts in the various fields. They certainly do not need pat and facile slogans. They should *think* and relate each new question to the biblical framework which also may be seen to be part of the grain of reality. They should enjoy the sense that a lot of questions are still unanswered, that we are still seeking.

An increasing body of technology will grow out of scientific discovery. All young people should be aware of the responsibilities and problems which this imposes on us all. A good example is considering the ethics of genetic development. Christians should think about how truth should direct action.

Where is this related thinking to take place? One student is at the public high school, and his family discusses these issues at great length. His own views are respected, and he is allowed to express various opinions. Basic principles are appealed to in a clear way, and it is seen that the working out of ideas, in practice, might take some time.

Another student, at the same school, has a family who cannot discuss these ideas meaningfully with him. Several adults at the church organize a weekend camp. He goes along and is able to ask his questions, listen to other students' questions, and discuss answers.

Yet another student is studying at a Christian high school. Teaching there is not a vehicle for indoctrinating the students with a single point of view but is a determination to teach science subjects as well as possible. The best and most interesting text on, say, biology is sought. Scientific clarity, high standards, and a text which is interesting to read are top considerations. The student needs a text, even at this stage, which is not a dull list of facts. His imagination needs to be touched. Again, the student has *not* grown out of the narration stage. He should read a chapter, or section, and be asked to tell it back in his own words in writing. This way he thinks, digests, questions, knows.

The high school should have many other reference books which will give different points of view in theoretical areas. This student, perhaps, will be able to have discussions relating the science to the humanities at school.

Whatever stage we get to, we should continue to wonder and appreciate. When a six-year-old and a sixty-year-old go outdoors to contemplate the skies at night, they both wonder, they each think their own thoughts. There are many questions, and it is exciting to search and beautiful to find.

Geography

"Now we're going on a journey. Let's go!"

These words are exciting at any age. Charlotte Mason urges us to keep this wide-eyed quality alive by avoiding a utilitarian approach to the teaching of geography. Her little children are alive to the countryside. Whatever the local environment is, they have explored it. For instance, they may have firsthand experience of climbing by a tumbling stream. They see how the water becomes calm and spreads as it enters a flat meadow. They are aware of the world around them. These children are used to being delighted with books. They only have lessons in the morning, so their attention is bright and alert. They are eager to have a story read which unfolds a descriptive panorama of some area or other. How dreary to try to remember the national product of Norway! But what fun to have one's imagination touched and to picture skating under Norwegian mountains, pausing to watch the ice-breaking ship enter the port with a catch of fish from the North Sea.

Charlotte Mason did not allow geography to be merely pictorial. The geography books of her day, she believed,

> . . . strip the unfortunate planet which has been assigned to us as our abode and environment of every trace of mystery and beauty. There is no longer anything to admire or to wonder at in this sweet world of ours.[16]

Therefore, she wrote her own geography books which described the places both at home and abroad in a systematic way but with the literary interest of personal discovery such as a traveler would experience. This was accompanied by thorough map work. Such an intimate and descriptive text could be "narrated" with interest by the student. These were places peopled by human beings, and the study related to history, literature, languages, art, etc. The students were also encouraged to record their graphic thinking by sketching what they had seen in their mind's eye.

A variety of books were chosen throughout the school, so that a child had a graphic and vivid picture of his own country, as well as world geography, by the end of his studies. This knowledge was to be related to current events when children were older. This was to be no mere textbook knowledge but should relate, for instance, to the news report they would read. Economic, political, and social factors were woven into this intimate relationship between the child and the physical world.

As always, the PNEU student would have exams at the end of the term. A small child might be asked to "Tell what you know about the city of London." There has been no revision, no cramming. The child was delighted to tell the adult many fascinating descriptions of London. An older child or teenager would accurately write a long essay on a detailed part of the syllabus which had been read perhaps four or five months before. The way these ordinary children retained their knowledge is a demonstration that this works.

Places and other people are interesting. Search for books which describe the "journey" vividly. Choose books which breathe life into real people living in these different places. There are many good stories that can relate to the study of geography. Let the children study good maps and enjoy recognizing the places they read about. Let them draw and describe the reading. Let older children relate current events to the geography studied at school. Intertwine it with history, literary descriptions, and books of adventure and travel. Some video material may also breathe life into the picture.

May the children know their planet!

Mathematics

The child in the PNEU school was helped by his habit of close attention when he was taught mathematics. However, Charlotte Mason felt that her particular insights about the philosophy of education had no distinctive contribution to make to the teaching methods used in this subject. She felt that the teaching of math depended on a teacher's ability to quicken interest and imagination. She thought that the child gifted in math should be able to forge ahead at his own pace, and the child less gifted should be helped to progress at his own rate. I think that she would certainly have welcomed methods which aided true understanding and practices which relate math to real life.

She had one fascinating comment on a metaphysical benefit derived from the concept of math.

> We take strong ground when we appeal to the beauty and truth of Mathematics; that, as Ruskin points out, two and two make four and cannot conceivably make five, is an inevitable law. It is a great thing to be brought into the presence of a law, of a whole system of laws, that exist without our concurrence—that two straight lines cannot enclose a space is a fact which we perceive, state, and act upon but cannot in any wise alter, should give to children the sense of limitation which is wholesome for all of us, and inspire that *sursum corda* which we should hear in all natural law.[17]

So she tells us that mathematics should be studied for its own sake, as well as to provide the root of knowledge out of which other branches of study depend.

I would add a few personal observations. Arithmetic should be grasped in steps which are mastered before the child is rushed on. What happens to the child who is away with tonsillitis the week borrowing is explained? Or to Tommy, who takes twice as long mastering the three times table as Sally? Surely, children must progress at an individual rate through a planned structure. Children often fail to grasp the basic concepts. They guess wildly. They think they are "dumb." They stop trying.

Were I teaching a child according to Charlotte Mason's plan for the school day, I would not spend too long on the arithmetic lesson. It would be given in the quiet first hours of the day, when the child can concentrate better than when tired. The child would have a grasp of number concepts verbally and in practice before formal work was introduced. Each step would be explained carefully. The child would tell back or verbalize the processes he was doing. There would be time for plenty of practice before progressing to a new step. The teaching would be as individual as possible. The child would feel confident before moving on.

As this child is not to be cooped up within the confines of the artificial world of the classroom for his whole day, he would see grown-ups applying arithmetic in real situations. Boys and girls see the value of taught skills in daily living. Cooking: first watching and then doing. Dressmaking: measuring and cutting fabric. Redecorating a bathroom: measuring the walls, estimating number of tiles, etc. Gardening: How many rows will fit in a certain space if they are each one foot apart? Shopping at the store: How many loaves of bread can I buy with this $5.00 bill? How much change should I have from the ice cream; am I being cheated? What time is the plane leaving? How many minutes are left?

If the parent is aware that the child is "lost" in math at school, he should take steps to build understanding. Ten minutes of math "games" a day can make a big difference; add, subtract, count. But danger lurks here. Is the child worn-out? Is he scared?

Today children are in a generation where they learn to handle the mechanical "brains" of computers. Personal computers, phones, and tablets, now a familiar sight in many family environments, can help a child develop the basic mathematical skills painlessly. A computer doesn't resent time spent endlessly testing a child in multiplication tables, and it is possible to buy many games and apps, created by skilled educators, which make many of the necessary, routine learning processes great fun.

Education is meant to serve the child. Study mathematics, and be sure that this is what it is doing. Relate the study to the child's needs. This has to include the requirements of society—for instance, levels of attainment required for a particular college, course, or examination.

Mathematics should be a "hands on" experience before the abstract shorthand of the mathematician is mastered. Ideally, it should relate to real life, to reality. It should be one more ordered piece of the puzzle. But beware! Many ordinary men and women look back upon math as irrelevant and a waste of time. We should try to see that it keeps its rightful place in the balance of the whole, and that we do not handicap a child in later life by making his early experiences of math irksome and difficult. As children progress and mature, they need to be prepared technically for the society in which we live.

Physical Development, Handicrafts

Charlotte Mason did not advise enclosing a child in an artificial environment, such as a classroom, for too much of the day. The whole afternoon was to be free for the child's own play. She held that the ideal was outdoor space where children ran, climbed trees, splashed, crawled, rode, explored, and played. Such children are strong little persons; they may exercise for five hours outside at their "play."

She also advises us to see that children learn other skills so that they master their bodies and relate them to their earth. She said they should be taught/allowed a variety of activities, such as swimming, rowing, riding, skating, and skiing.

She did not despise organized games. She felt that the team experience taught good lessons of cooperation and loyalty, but that they should not be of central importance. Her pupils loved the games in which all of them were involved equally. She had little time for the purely competitive game, designed to bring one child to glory and the rest to disappointment.

If children had to be confined indoors, she advised gymnastics and other physical activities. I feel sure she would have been glad to see the modern sports center near my home where on a dark, cold British winter night people of all ages can engage in a variety of activities.

She would have been sympathetic to the abnormality of the surroundings many urban children grow up in, and would have approved of schools which include parklike areas for play. Another delight would be open-plan areas for children inside those schools. After lessons in a quiet ordered room, a substitute for freedom of home and garden can be the possibility of choosing to spend time in woodworking, an art area, a kitchen, a library, etc.

She would have welcomed the camping programs that get children out of cities into a natural setting.

She would have us think of nature as one of the basic factors in a person's life. Teaching New Testament stories to inner-city children is surely Christian. But it is also Christian, for instance, to take these same children out of the city regularly by bus. Let them have the richness of God's nature. Let them open their eyes to beauty, even if it doesn't hit them all at once. Let them run and jump until they are hungry and exhausted. Feed them well physically, but do not forget their whole need.

Help youngsters plan a bicycle trip, maybe taking lightweight camping gear. Go as a family or together in some other group relationship.

We are told by Charlotte Mason that it is not a luxury to become—and stay—fit. We and the children are to see it as a duty! We cannot be prepared to serve if we are unfit and breathless soldiers.

Children will enjoy using their bodies actively in many ways, both in free time and as part of an organized schedule. They should learn that it is a part of life to regulate time and responsibilities so that one is living within one's limits. They should know something of the rhythm of hard work and relaxation. They should experience the new vigor brought to a hard task when one stays exercised and rested physically. They should want to be as strong and well as possible so as to be useful in hard service.

The child was also to have as rich a variety of skills in crafts as possible. Charlotte Mason was ahead of her time when she advocated that girls and boys should share the same activities both physically and in handicraft and work. They should be able to sew, cook, knit, embroider, and work with clay, wood, and metal. They should also know how to grow plants and benefit from having an animal to care for. Remember, in this area, that Charlotte Mason pictured many young children being taught by their mothers or a teacher at home. They would then share in "real" activities rather than an arranged program. They would observe and share in home duties. They would have a longer time to either play or carry on with a handicraft as a hobby out of their free choice. A home bubbling with life-activity is more a part of reality. Handicrafts and work are seen within a meaningful environment.

I met a young woman who was to teach urban youngsters home economics. Their inner-city school had almost given up on some of these children with social and learning problems. She obtained permission to take her class out of the school to a home especially prepared by a local church for a period of half a day per class. This way, over one hundred young teenagers spent a half day in the "house" each week. She would bring a pile of ironing and an iron into the kitchen—not quite the teacher image! She became a *person* to them, and she accepted them as *persons*. In fact, she took them at face value; she refused to look at their records or to be impressed by their previous failures or delinquent acts. They cooked real meals and learned about nutrition bit by bit as they talked. They grew things in the garden and sewed for themselves and for the house. Friends would bring in babies and toddlers, and the teenagers loved watching and then playing with the children. They would read stories to a two-year-old, and then end up discussing what fathers can do with their babies, as they sat at the kitchen table with cups of coffee. Children who had stopped cooperating long before loved it all, had new ideas, talked, and asked. They often started writing cookbooks, and sometimes other creative writing would follow.

I think this would have delighted Charlotte Mason. She would only be sad that the one morning could not be stretched to more days. She knew that such youngsters would delight in a really good book read aloud to them. "Feed their minds," she would admonish us. Nurture the whole person.

The life of education has to include the *whole* of our humanness. We need to relate as persons to the God who is there, to be nourished with good ideas through books, art, music, history, literature, etc. We need to relate to other persons, to know and be known. We need the beauty of nature, and we are made to respond creatively in speech, music, through art, etc. We need to know the limits of law and yet the freedom of our separate choices.

Let me quote Charlotte Mason, who said it better than I can.

Children should have relations with earth and water, should run and leap, ride and swim, should establish the relation of maker to material in as many kinds as may be; should have dear and intimate relations with persons, through present intercourse, through tale or poem, picture or statue; through flint arrow-head or modern motor-car: beast and bird, herb and tree, they must have familiar acquaintance with. Other peoples and their languages must not be strange to them. Above all they should find that most intimate and highest of all Relationships—the fulfillment of their being [their relationship with God].

This is not a bewildering programme, because, in all these and more directions, children have affinities; and a human being does not fill his place in the universe without putting out tendrils of attachment in the directions proper to him. We must get rid of the notion that to learn the "three R's" or the Latin grammar well, a child should learn these and nothing else. It is as true for children as for ourselves that, the wider the range of interests, the more intelligent is the apprehension of each.[18]

6

The Way of the Will, Reason, and the Unity of the Whole

WE ARE COMING TO THE END of the "short synopsis" of education which Charlotte Mason wrote as the basis of principle and operation. We have now arrived at points 15–18, which cover the will, reason, and the unity of all truth and action, which Christianity holds as our foundation of life and action.

Throughout this book I have included relevant comments on these aspects, as I wanted to tie them into the rest of our considerations. However, it would be worthwhile to focus attention on them specifically once again.

When our children first attended their PNEU school, they each came home with a lovely brooch to wear on their school sweaters. In a circle was a flying skylark. Surrounding it were the words, "I am, I can, I ought, I will."

This PNEU motto, if learned, believed, and practiced, is a key to human life. It embodies the basic Christian concepts and principles, if understood within the whole context of biblical teaching and common-sense human experience.

"I Am"

The person should know about his worth, his unique place as a creature made to have a relationship with God. He understands who he is, his ability to choose, that he matters, that he is accepted and valued. He should like himself, even love himself. He is realistic; he accepts his own limitations, and knows that he can be creative within them. Having liked and accepted himself, he will go on to have the basis for liking and accepting his neighbor. Knowing that God has loved and served him, he will know that it is right to love, accept, and serve others. This security is fostered by the child's *human* relationships, more than *words* about God to begin with. He should be with people who treat him with respect, politeness, truth. This includes the parent/teacher's not pretending to know everything or acting as if he has arrived and is morally or spiritually perfect. If we are truthful about our own knowledge/intellectual limitations, this fresh air of truth and openness will help the child accept himself. It will help him strive for what is right and good. We prefer the company of others like ourselves to the intimidation of a superman or woman who makes us feel rotten.

As a Christian, I know that non-Christian philosophy can never provide the happy secure understanding of who I actually am. I might be ugly, not too brilliant, with a low salary, and aging, and yet have a sweet assurance that I am so valuable that Jesus would have come to rescue me from the fate of a fallen planet. This may give me liberty to enjoy all the positive aspects of myself, my relationships, my responsibilities—and to be *rich in life*.

We hinder the child's assurance of his worth—"just as I am"—when we set up artificial development schedules into which we try to cram the child grade by grade. The program then matters more than the child. We push the "slow" and bore the "quick." We ignore the living mind. We allow peer pressure in this materialistic and godless culture to become like a row of vultures, judging the child with beady eyes. The teacher and the school report can join this gauntlet of judgment through which the quivering child has to march.

We really do have to try to get away from our success-orientated society where people bolster their selfish egos by comparing their achievements as being better than someone else's. "My job/salary/education/status is better than yours" is an ugly and wrong thought. It is so easy to make slaves of children for these same selfish and misguided reasons. "My Johnny learned to read at four, plays the violin, writes computer programs, and is on the Little League team." But is it *good* for Johnny? Is it *right?* Who is kidding whom? And will he still like himself if, after ten years of pushing, he flunks a course, or doesn't go to college, or becomes lame and has to be last physically instead of first? Where is the *time* for Johnny to flower as he *is*—developing a unity of self and aims?

"I am!" I am a person of unique worth. I can have a relationship with the eternal God and the whole of reality of which he has created me to be a part. I live in a fallen world, and it affects me in different ways. I expect and understand that. I can be realistic about the truth about myself. I don't feel guilty about enjoying the whole of life, be it a beach at sunset, sexual enjoyment in marriage, food, a good book, a play, or work. *I am.* I am finite, can't know it all or do it all—but I am God's child. I am dependent. Yet, he trusts me, lets me have responsibility and abundant *life.* I accept my freedom within his laws. My perspectives are not limited by this side of death. I am born to live eternally, and my destination is not limited by my college education, my salary, or what other people think. I am, in a sense, alone before God. He gave me my own separate life, and he will direct me into the right path for *me*. That is my aim, my ambition.

"I Can"

Yes, I believe in myself in a balanced, realistic way. I tackle appropriate goals with confidence. Whether they be small (learning to tie my shoelaces at six), big (learning to live with my husband/wife in "real" life), hard (making a creative life when there are severe limitations, like being paralyzed), or fun (planning to walk around the coast of the Isle of Wight), "secular" or "spiritual," I know that "I can." Some things are a snap, others need perseverance and the help of the Holy Spirit. Sometimes I set (or somebody else sets) goals that aren't right for *me*. But having said that, you could divide people into those who feel they can, and those who assume they can't. (They turn and run, stop, don't try, etc.) Beware, all adults. Build up children by helping them turn into "can" people!

"I Ought"

We live in the century of "I want." Many actually believe that "anything goes." Study the Bible to see what are the "oughts." Gently apply this framework. It is the only one to teach children. We lead them into a pasture. We study them so that we won't make the horrible mistake of "punishing" them for behavior proper to their age. (Babies wriggle, two-year-olds cling to possessions, six-year-olds may be clumsy and spill milk, nine-year-olds may be overpressured and unable to organize the details of their lives, etc.) We are to *serve* them, love them. Part of this love is to live under the authority of God and his word. We do not impose arbitrary standards. It is not, "What do I/you want?" but, "*What is right?*" and then, "I ought."

"Choose you this day whom ye will serve." There are two services open to us all, the service of God, (including that of man) and the service of self. If our aim is just to get on, "to do ourselves well," to get all possible ease, luxury and pleasure out of our lives, we are serving self and for the service of self no act of will is required. Our appetites and desires are always at hand to spur us into the necessary exertions. But if we serve God and our neighbour, we have to be always on the watch to choose between the ideas that present themselves.[1]

"I Will"

Having clarified what is right, we realize that we are able to *choose* what is right. "I will do it, even though I don't feel like it/it is hard/everybody else isn't doing it." The adult can ease right-doing by making basic patterns habitual. Consider this: Would you be willing to cut off the brainwashing of the media to help the child? No or little TV? Giving your home so much vitality, life, through your creative time and effort that it becomes the "center of gravity" in the child's life? This means it has more influence than the peer pressure. In this way, a child may be liberated from the spineless atmosphere which assumes that one can't decide what "I will" do based on what is *right*, rather than what I am pushed into against my better judgment by others or by circumstances.

"I am, I can, I ought, I will."

Of course, we need to fail sometimes. This helps us to aim realistically or to learn aspects of truth (about ourselves or the situation).

Paul adds a note here for our aid, "I can do everything through [Christ] who gives me strength" (Phil. 4:13).

Charlotte Mason gives us a plan which is beautifully balanced. The children have certain set tasks so that they learn the basic skills. Their minds are nourished; they are put in touch with the whole of reality. They have structure, and yet they are given time (half the day) for freedom. (This was up to the age of thirteen years in the PNEU school, without homework.) They can develop their own affinities. They can "be," imagine, play, ponder, create, read. They can move, be noisy, quiet, social, or alone. This growing time produces integrated people who understand their own limitations, desires, interests, gifts, and tendencies. One person will end up in the garage tinkering with an old motor, another will be playing with toddlers, another will draw pictures and tell stories, while yet another thinks of ways to earn money.

The children are respected and accepted as valid persons. But they are not left on the island of their own limited resources. Through careful choice, they are nourished with the best we human beings have to offer: mind is introduced to mind, child to nature and activities.

Pray that our children may be so educated in a total life that they are enabled to have clear, realistic, and true thinking and action based on thought and principle. May they be strong personalities, free of self and external pressures so that they will have the power to do what is right.

Again, I will quote principle number 18, rather than rehash it here:

We should allow no separation to grow up between the intellectual and "spiritual" life of children; but should teach them that the divine Spirit has constant access to their spirits, and is their continual helper in all the interests, duties and joys of life.[2]

Last week I was walking across a hilltop ridge of the South Downs. To the south, the English Channel glinted with sun; to the east, the ridge of hills beckoned with clean, sensual lines. Northward, the rolling farmland extended in all directions. The sweet spring air was not silent. The song of a soaring skylark accompanied our walk. Sweet and clear, the skylark "flies the highest and sings the sweetest."

The motto, "I am, I can, I ought, I will" makes a circle, a perimeter, inside of which my human life may be lived with joy and fullness. There is song, lightness, spontaneity. There is the possibility of attaining height proper to one's self. True fullness of life cannot come without godly perimeters. The fish in the sea, the bird in the air, the child in the garden with his friends. We may all soar, sing, live when we stay within our proper framework.

Abundant Life

The children rush out into the summer sunshine. After an enthusiastic scamper, they divide into little groups to pursue serious and happy self-appointed projects. Three little boys start building a camp; one girl has taken out a blanket, pillows, and snack, and has curled up under a tree with a new book to read. Two young children have brought out their toy cars, and raked the gravel into roads along which the cars are now driving. An elaborate play (describing events) is being acted out cheerfully. A couple of girls have dressed up, and are now deciding whether to play that they are traveling to Australia or whether to act out a play. Childhood!

Somewhere else, a family has set out for the day, with picnics packed on their bikes. A route has been planned, and the children bicycle away joyfully. The birds sing, and the family's spirits start lifting.

A boy is in the library, carefully selecting a few more books to read. He rustles the pages thoughtfully and scans the chapter headings. He is like someone anticipating a good meal when hungry. He is looking forward to reading.

In the classroom, the children are sitting in a circle with their eyes on the teacher. They are relaxed and attentive, captivated with the "story" being read to them. When she stops, there is a stir. "Please, could we have some more? No? Oh, *please.*" The children enjoy taking turns telling back the story, and they happily settle down to drawing a picture about what they have heard.

Here we have another class in the urban center of a city. These children, too, have responded very deeply to the excellent material being spread before them in the form of a well-read and captivating book. They hang on to the story, and their comments are acute and thoughtful. They receive the matter and digest it using their good minds. Dull eyes become alert; interest grows.

Out in the country, yet another group of children are being given three weeks to enjoy the freedom and joy of nature. They are usually cooped up for one reason or another, so at first they find everything strangely exciting. Nature itself is full of the unknown and amazing. They splash in the stream more like five-year-olds than fourteen-year-olds. They pull up plants to see the roots, and start back from a grass snake. They enjoy feeding animals and start asking questions. *Why? How?* It's a new world.

Around a table a group (family, students, or friends) have finished a meal. They don't get up because the discussion has become quite lively. They are talking about what they have been reading in relationship to the day's news report or ideas they have encountered. They are thinking, expressing themselves, and slowly they come to some conclusions of their own.

At the piano, two people are composing a new song. There is laughter, some frustration, and persevering effort. Soon the song takes shape.

As well as these free-time activities, work must be accomplished. The "oughts" are accepted and done. The dishes are washed, the money earned, the garden weeded, the spelling rules learned, the math page mastered. People act individually at times, and at other times in groups. They shouldn't be afraid to express love, affection. They should serve each other's needs. When they do wrong, they are to admit it, say sorry, and try again.

All of these happenings, plus countless more, could serve to describe the principles of education outlined in this book.

Is all of this a kind of fairy tale? Do we have to accept instead the "real life" of fear, failure, boredom, suppression, conformity, selfishness, laziness, pride, materialism? Do we say it is "more real" that children should be subjected to garbage, trivia, horror, false thinking, and wrong living? Does neglect toughen up the child for adulthood? Do we give in to peer pressure which expects the false, wrong, and empty behavior which is the "done thing?" Or do we slap the children's hands with a sharp, No, no! and then give them the emptiness of law without abundant life—no heart, song, or joy?

Someone will react, "But this sort of education, atmosphere, discipline, and life is impossible." Why? "Oh, parents/homes/ teachers/schools aren't like that. Children aren't like that."

Well, I disagree—and I agree.

No parent/home/child/teacher/school has an all-round 100 percent wholeness. We all have limitations and problems. But I must never think that it is everything or nothing.

Perhaps I'd like to live in the country, but I don't. Well, maybe I can get the family to a park two times a week, and out to the country once every two weeks.

Maybe I have to send my child to a not-so-good school. Well, maybe we can read one or two good books together aloud. If you can't give them *everything*, give them *something*.

Maybe you are teaching in a regular public school. Well, maybe you can apply *some* of the ideas. Try talking at them much, much less. Read to the children out of a few interesting books. Try to adapt *some* of the ideas. Different teachers can do different things. Open doors; care for the persons who are the children; stick by biblical principles of what is important and what isn't. Try to let their minds work on good material.

Let us be challenged to change our homes, our churches, and maybe our schools. We need to study children as they are, as they *could be*. We need to know truth and the wholeness of life.

But please, let us join Charlotte Mason in her deep burden for the underprivileged. Let us not confine our total efforts to our *own* children in our *own* homes or neighborhoods.

There are so many neglected children today. Some are suffering from lack of family, caring, time, structure, true education, etc. Others are in inner cities, and they seem "barely human." Do we care? Will we pass by on the other side? One day we will stand before God Almighty, and he will accept what we have done for our own children. But who will care for the "other children"? Will somebody let them be persons in God's world too? Who will serve them? Charlotte Mason had deep joy when she saw the results of children in the poor schools of industrial slums responding to her program as had those with more favored family backgrounds.

We must be challenged today. Yes, as a parent, my first responsibility is my family. But as a Christian, as a citizen, I must think about what else is my responsibility—who else needs me/us.

The education has to be self-education. The child's mind is as good as the adult's mind. Our task is to provide nourishment. We neither undervalue the child nor the knowledge. We provide a personal relationship, the source material, and the framework for this growth. *He* does his *own* learning, living, responding.

There can be no greater vocation in life than the family responsibility of sharing life with the growing child. The school is an extension of our home. These are hard days, in many ways, for rightful living. It doesn't "just happen." Stop and think. Get priorities right. And remember, education is ongoing. We, too, are learning, growing, living. We are to "become as little children."

And so let me close this book.

Come, child.
I respect you, you are a person.
Come with me.
You belong on this planet
You are to inherit,
You are to understand.
Look. Look, and you will see.
Enjoy this day: the sun, the grass, your friends.
Listen—we will read God's word.
We are his sheep, he is our Shepherd.
Grow! Flourish! Be master!
Let us do what we ought.
Let us choose the right!
Let us be brothers and sisters, together.
The bored wake up,
The failures find a new spring,
The sinful start again.
Come, little child,
I will listen, I will learn, too—
Let us enjoy abundant LIFE!

Notes

Chapter 1: What Is Education?
1. From the motto of Charlotte Mason College, Ambleside, England.

Chapter 2: "Children Are Born Persons"
1. Charlotte Mason, *A Philosophy of Education* (Carol Stream, IL: Tyndale, 1989), 65, 66.
2. Mason, *A Philosophy of Education*, 2–3 (italics mine).
3. Mason, *A Philosophy of Education*, 34.
4. Mason, *A Philosophy of Education*, 35–36.
5. Charlotte Mason, *Home Education* (Carol Stream, IL: Tyndale, 1989), 187.
6. Charlotte Mason, *School Education* (Carol Stream, IL: Tyndale, 1989), 36–37.
7. Charlotte Mason, *Home Education*, 176–77.
8. Mason, *Home Education*, 227–28.
9. Mason, *Home Education*, 225–26.
10. I would add: "and who don't know any children personally." This is a greater problem now than ever before. The "educated" adult has usually been out of real touch with children for many years.
11. Italics mine. Mason, *Home Education*, 229.
12. Good lists of "living books" can be found in Gladys M. Hunt, *Honey for a Child's Heart*, 4th ed. (Grand Rapids, MI: Zondervan, 2002).
13. Charlotte Mason, *A Philosophy of Education*, 26.
14. Mason, *A Philosophy of Education*, 28–29.
15. Marva Collins's accomplishments have been well-documented and are to be much admired.

Chapter 3: Authority and Freedom
1. Charlotte Mason, *A Philosophy of Education* (Carol Stream, IL: Tyndale, 1989), 46.

2. Mason, *A Philosophy of Education*, 64.
3. Charlotte Mason, *School Education* (Carol Stream, IL: Tyndale, 1989), 21–22.
4. Mason, *School Education*, 23–24.
5. Mason, *Home Education* (Carol Stream, IL: Tyndale, 1989), 188.
6. Mason, *Home Education*, 162.
7. Mason, *Home Education*, 163–64.

Chapter 4: A New Perspective
1. Charlotte Mason, *Home Education* (Carol Stream, IL: Tyndale, 1989), 98–100.
2. Charlotte Mason, *A Philosophy of Education* (Carol Stream, IL: Tyndale, 1989), xxix.
3. Mason, *A Philosophy of Education*, xxix.
4. Francis A. Schaeffer, *A Christian Manifesto* (Wheaton, IL: Crossway, 1981), 20–21.
5. Mason, *A Philosophy of Education*, 81.
6. Mason, *A Philosophy of Education*, 82.
7. Mason, *A Philosophy of Education*, 101.
8. Mason, *A Philosophy of Education*, 109.

Chapter 5: Education: A Science of Relationships
1. Charlotte Mason, *A Philosophy of Education* (Carol Stream, IL: Tyndale, 1989), 158.
2. Mason, *A Philosophy of Education*, 160.
3. Charlotte Mason, *Home Education* (Carol Stream, IL: Tyndale, 1989), 351.
4. Charlotte Mason, *Formation of Character* (Carol Stream, IL: Tyndale, 1989), 256.
5. Mason, *Formation of Character*, 256–57.
6. Francis A. Schaeffer, *A Christian Manifesto* (Wheaton, IL: Crossway, 1981), 19–20.
7. Mason, *A Philosophy of Education*, 178.
8. Mason, *A Philosophy of Education*, 179.
9. Mason, *A Philosophy of Education*, 178.
10. Mason, *Home Education*, 288.
11. Mason, *A Philosophy of Education*, 184.
12. Mason, *A Philosophy of Education*, 183.
13. Mason, *A Philosophy of Education*, 186–87.
14. Mason, *A Philosophy of Education*, 190.
15. Mason, *A Philosophy of Education*, 191–92.

16. Mason, *A Philosophy of Education*, 224.
17. Mason, *A Philosophy of Education*, 230–31.
18. Mason, *School Education* (Carol Stream, IL: Tyndale, 1989), 209.

Chapter 6: The Way of the Will, Reason, and the Unity of the Whole
1. Charlotte Mason, *A Philosophy of Education* (Carol Stream, IL: Tyndale, 1989), 134–35.
2. Mason, *A Philosophy of Education*, xxxi.

Resource List

THERE ARE VARIOUS EDITIONS of Charlotte Mason's series available online from various publishers.

Mason, Charlotte. *Home Education.* Vol. 1. Ambleside, 1886.

Mason, Charlotte. *Parents and Children.* Vol. 2. Ambleside, 1897.

Mason, Charlotte. *School Education.* Vol. 3. Ambleside, n.d.

Mason, Charlotte. *Ourselves.* Vol. 4. Ambleside, 1904.

Mason, Charlotte. *Formation of Character.* Vol. 5. Ambleside, 1905.

Mason, Charlotte. *A Philosophy of Education.* Vol. 6. Ambleside, 1923.

———

Cholmondeley, Essex. *The Story of Charlotte Mason.* Cambridge, UK: The Lutterworth Press, 2021.

Cooper, Elaine, ed. *When Children Love to Learn.* Wheaton, IL: Crossway, 2004.

———

Helpful Curriculum Resources:

Ambleside Online: https://www.amblesideonline.org/
Charlotte Mason Institute website: https://charlottemasoninstitute
.org/alveary-membership/

———

Helpful Resources for Reading with Children and Young People:

Butler, Dorothy. *Babies Need Books*. 3rd Edition. Penguin, 1995.
Butler, Dorothy. *From Five to Eight: Vital Years for Reading*. Bodley Head Children's, 1986.
Hunt, Gladys. *Honey for a Child's Heart*. 4th Edition. Grand Rapids, MI: Zondervan, 2002.
Hunt, Gladys, and Barbara Hampton. *Honey for a Teen's Heart: Using Books to Communicate with Your Teens*. Grand Rapids, MI: Zondervan, 2002.
Wilson, Elizabeth. *Books Children Love*. Revised Edition. Wheaton, IL: Crossway, 2002.

About Child Light Limited

CHILD LIGHT LIMITED is a UK registered charity that has existed in its current legal form since 1994. An earlier Child Light Foundation was established to promote Charlotte Mason based education as a result of the widespread interest generated by the publication of *For the Children's Sake* by Susan Schaeffer Macaulay in 1984. Over the years, Child Light's activities have included speaking at and organizing conferences and publishing. Other important titles have included *When Children Love to Learn: A Practical Application of Charlotte Mason's Philosophy for Today*, edited by Elaine Cooper (Crossways Books, 2004) and *The Story of Charlotte Mason* by Essex Cholmondeley (The Lutterworth Press, 2021).

In September 2007 Childlight founded a school in Cambridge, United Kingdom. Heritage School is a model school that seeks to demonstrate and advocate a more humane vision of education for the twenty-first century. Its work is inspired by the principles and educational methods put forward by Charlotte Mason and the PNEU (Parent's National Education Union), which she founded in the late nineteenth century.

www.childlight.org.uk

Index

on authority, 66–67; belief
that right habits should be
established in childhood,
64–65; on boys and girls
sharing the same activities,
177; on children's relations
with earth and water, 178–79;
on corporal punishment, 74;
on the creative development
of language, 150; curriculum
of, 117; death of, 21; education of, 20; on education
(educational philosophy/plan
of), 22–23, 27, 117, 127–28,
154–55, 168, 186; on encouraging creativity, 159–60; on
the family, 95–97; and her
search for true education,
81–83; on the ideal world for
children, 111; on kindergarten, 75–76; on leading the
child to art, 156–57; lectures
on the subject of education,
20–21; on mathematics,
173; on narration, 45–46;
on obedience, 77; opening of
the House of Education, 21;
passionate belief that children
are persons, 20; on personal
influence used to manipulate
boys and girls, 90–91; plan
for teaching, reading, and
number work, 44–45; on the
practicality of God's moral
law, 89; rejection of the idea
that children as persons need
molding, 30; rejection of the
utilitarian view of education,
29–30; respect of for a child's
mind, 134–35; on routines

for children, 105–7; on
satisfying the minds of young
persons, 49–50; on schools,
40–41, 42; sharing of the
good things in life with children, 31–32; short synopsis of
the educational philosophy of,
83–87; on textbooks, 137; on
young mothers and allowing
children to play, 163–64
mathematics, 128, 172–75; as a
"hands on" experience, 175
mind, the, 126
morals, importance of, 144–49
moral law, 89, 94, 95
music, 160–63; musical creativity,
161–62; in worship, 162–63

narration, 45–46
National Society of Parents, 21
notebooks, 153

parents, 16; and the exercise of
self-restraint, 78–79; and the
mistake of thinking chil-
dren have to be twaddled
at, 32–33, 136; need of to
evaluate their priorities, 25;
responsibility toward children, 92; and taking a child
into confidence, 77–78
Parents' National Education Union
(PNEU) schools, 21, 53, 56,
120, 122, 139, 149, 159,
160–61, 172; curriculum of,
144; motto of, 181–82; nature
walks and nature notebooks of,
165–66; in Sussex, 58; three
terms of, 157
Paul, 47, 48, 121, 185